JOSEPH BRANT

NORTH AMERICAN INDIANS OF ACHIEVEMENT

JOSEPH BRANT
Mohawk Chief

▼▼▼

Jonathan Bolton and Claire Wilson

Senior Consulting Editor
W. David Baird
Howard A. White Professor of History
Pepperdine University

CHELSEA HOUSE PUBLISHERS

Philadelphia

FRONTISPIECE   American artist Charles Willson Peale's portrait of Joseph Brant. The image was painted during Brant's 1797 trip to Philadelphia.

ON THE COVER   This painting is based on a portrait rendered by American artist Gilbert Stuart in 1786, while Joseph Brant was in London. Brant is dressed in Indian finery, including a feather headdress, a headband of metal rings, and a shell necklace. According to Brant's daughter, Stuart's portrait was the truest likeness of her father ever painted.

Chelsea House Publishers
EDITOR-IN-CHIEF   Richard S. Papale
MANAGING EDITOR   Karyn Gullen Browne
COPY CHIEF   Philip Koslow
PICTURE EDITOR   Adrian G. Allen
ART DIRECTOR   Maria Epes
ASSISTANT ART DIRECTOR   Howard Brotman
MANUFACTURING DIRECTOR   Gerald Levine
SYSTEMS MANAGER   Lindsey Ottman
PRODUCTION MANAGER   Joseph Romano
PRODUCTION COORDINATOR   Marie Claire Cebrián

North American Indians of Achievement
SENIOR EDITOR   Liz Sonneborn

Staff for JOSEPH BRANT
COPY EDITOR   Ian Wilker
EDITORIAL ASSISTANT   Michele Berezansky
DESIGNER   Debora Smith
PICTURE RESEARCHER   Melanie Sanford
COVER ILLUSTRATION   Shelley Pritchett

3 5 7 9 8 6 4 2

Library of Congress Cataloging-in-Publication Data

Bolton, Jonathan.
Joseph Brant: Mohawk chief/by Jonathan Bolton and Claire Wilson.
   p. cm.—(North American Indians of achievement)
Includes index.
Summary: Examines the life of the Mohawk chief, missionary, and statesman who led his people on the side of the British in the Revolutionary War.
ISBN 0-7910-1709-5
1. Brant, Joseph. 1742–1807—Juvenile literature. 2. Mohawk Indians—Biography—Juvenile literature. 3. Indians of North America—Wars—1750–1815—Juvenile literature. [1. Brant, Joseph, 1742–1807. 2. Mohawk Indians—Biography. 3. Indians of North America—Biography.] I. Wilson, Claire. II. Title. III. Series
E99.M8W58 1992   91-38917
973'.0497502—dc20   CIP
[B]   AC

CONTENTS

NORTH AMERICAN INDIANS OF ACHIEVEMENT

BLACK HAWK
Sac Rebel

JOSEPH BRANT
Mohawk Chief

COCHISE
Apache Chief

CRAZY HORSE
Sioux War Chief

CHIEF GALL
Sioux War Chief

GERONIMO
Apache Warrior

HIAWATHA
Founder of the Iroquois
Confederacy

CHIEF JOSEPH
Nez Perce Leader

PETER MACDONALD
Former Chairman of the Navajo
Nation

WILMA MANKILLER
Principal Chief of the Cherokees

OSCEOLO
Seminole Rebel

QUANAH PARKER
Comanche Chief

KING PHILIP
Wampanoag Rebel

**POCAHONTAS AND CHIEF
POWHATAN**
Leaders of the Powhatan Tribes

PONTIAC
Ottawa Rebel

RED CLOUD
Sioux War Chief

WILL ROGERS
Cherokee Entertainer

SEQUOYAH
Inventor of the Cherokee Alphabet

SITTING BULL
Chief of the Sioux

TECUMSEH
Shawnee Rebel

JIM THORPE
Sac and Fox Athlete

SARAH WINNEMUCCA
Northern Paiute Writer and
Diplomat

Other titles in preparation

ON INDIAN LEADERSHIP

by W. David Baird
Howard A. White Professor of History
Pepperdine University

Authoritative utterance is in thy mouth, perception is in thy heart, and thy tongue is the shrine of justice," the ancient Egyptians said of their king. From him, the Egyptians expected authority, discretion, and just behavior. Homer's *Iliad* suggests that the Greeks demanded somewhat different qualities from their leaders: justice and judgment, wisdom and counsel, shrewdness and cunning, valor and action. It is not surprising that different people living at different times should seek different qualities from the individuals they looked to for guidance. By and large, a people's requirements for leadership are determined by two factors: their culture and the unique circumstances of the time and place in which they live.

Before the late 15th century, when non-Indians first journeyed to what is now North America, most Indian tribes were not ruled by a single person. Instead, there were village chiefs, clan headmen, peace chiefs, war chiefs, and a host of other types of leaders, each with his or her own specific duties. These influential people not only decided political matters but also helped shape their tribe's social, cultural, and religious life. Usually, Indian leaders held their positions because they had won the respect of their peers. Indeed, if a leader's followers at any time decided that he or she was out of step with the will of the people, they felt free to look to someone else for advice and direction.

Thus, the greatest achievers in traditional Indian communities were men and women of extraordinary talent. They were not only skilled at navigating the deadly waters of tribal politics and cultural customs but also able to, directly or indirectly, make a positive and significant difference in the daily life of their followers.

From the beginning of their interaction with Native Americans, non-Indians failed to understand these features of Indian leadership. Early European explorers and settlers merely assumed that Indians had the same relationship with their leaders as non-Indians had with their kings and queens. European monarchs generally inherited their positions and ruled large nations however they chose, often with little regard for the desires or needs of their subjects. As a result, the settlers of Jamestown saw Pocahontas as a "princess" and Pilgrims dubbed Wampanoag leader Metacom "King Philip," envisioning them in roles very different from those in which their own people placed them.

As more and more non-Indians flocked to North America, the nature of Indian leadership gradually began to change. Influential Indians no longer had to take on the often considerable burden of pleasing only their own people; they also had to develop a strategy of dealing with the non-Indian newcomers. In a rapidly changing world, new types of Indian role models with new ideas and talents continually emerged. Some were warriors; others were peacemakers. Some held political positions within their tribes; others were writers, artists, religious prophets, or athletes. Although the demands of Indian leadership altered from generation to generation, several factors that determined which Indian people became prominent in the centuries after first contact remained the same.

Certain personal characteristics distinguished these Indians of achievement. They were intelligent, imaginative, practical, daring, shrewd, uncompromising, ruthless, and logical. They were constant in friendships, unrelenting in hatreds, affectionate with their relatives, and respectful to their God or gods. Of course, no single Native American leader embodied all these qualities, nor these qualities only. But it was these characteristics that allowed them to succeed.

The special skills and talents that certain Indians possessed also brought them to positions of importance. The life of Hiawatha, the legendary founder of the powerful Iroquois Confederacy, displays the value that oratorical ability had for many Indians in power.

The biography of Cochise, the 19th-century Apache chief, illustrates that leadership often required keen diplomatic skills not only in transactions among tribespeople but also in hardheaded negotiations with non-Indians. For others, such as Mohawk Joseph Brant and Navajo Peter MacDonald, a non-Indian education proved advantageous in their dealings with other peoples.

Sudden changes in circumstance were another crucial factor in determining who became influential in Indian communities. King Philip in the 1670s and Geronimo in the 1880s both came to power when their people were searching for someone to lead them into battle against white frontiersmen who had forced upon them a long series of indignities. Seeing the rising discontent of Indians of many tribes in the 1810s, Tecumseh and his brother, the Shawnee prophet Tenskwatawa, proclaimed a message of cultural revitalization that appealed to thousands. Other Indian achievers recognized cooperation with non-Indians as the most advantageous path during their lifetime. Sarah Winnemucca in the late 19th century bridged the gap of understanding between her people and their non-Indian neighbors through the publication of her autobiography *Life Among the Piutes*. Olympian Jim Thorpe in the early 20th century championed the assimilationist policies of the U.S. government and, with his own successes, demonstrated the accomplishments Indians could make in the non-Indian world. And Wilma Mankiller, principal chief of the Cherokees, continues to fight successfully for the rights of her people through the courts and through negotiation with federal officials.

Leadership among Native Americans, just as among all other peoples, can be understood only in the context of culture and history. But the centuries that Indians have had to cope with invasions of foreigners in their homelands have brought unique hardships and obstacles to the Native American individuals who most influenced and inspired others. Despite these challenges, there has never been a lack of Indian men and women equal to these tasks. With such strong leaders, it is no wonder that Native Americans remain such a vital part of this nation's cultural landscape.

1

A MOHAWK AT THE KING'S COURT

In early January 1776, the merchant ship *Adamant* entered the harbor at Falmouth, England. Its crew and passengers were relieved to see the bustling port city after 40 days at sea. They were also surprised at the large, staring crowds that were lined up on the piers to greet them.

Most of the curious onlookers were gathered to get a glimpse of just one of the ship's passengers—Ethan Allen. Allen was the leader of a force of rebellious American colonists who were battling for independence from the British government. In May 1775, his soldiers, the Green Mountain Boys, had attacked and captured Fort Ticonderoga, a British stronghold in the colony of New York. The rebels then attempted to repeat their success at the fortified city of Montreal in Canada. This time, however, the tide turned against them. The band was captured, and Allen was shipped off to Great Britain to stand trial for high treason.

While waiting for Allen to disembark from the *Adamant*, the citizens of Falmouth witnessed an unexpected sight that intrigued them even more than the possibility of a look at the famed rebel. Down the gangway proceeded the entourage of Sir Guy Johnson,

A silver gorget (metal collar) that King George III gave to Joseph Brant during Brant's 1776 trip to London.

the acting colonial superintendent of Indian affairs for all of North America. Among the group were two odd-looking men wearing strange outfits. They had feathers in their hair, wore colorful sashes and large silver ornaments on their bodies, and carried formidable hatchets and knives in their belts—not the everyday garb of the average British citizen. The men were Joseph Brant and John Hill Oteronyente, Mohawk Indians whose tribal leaders had charged them with the task of delivering a message to George III, the king of England.

The two young Indians were enjoying their assignment thus far. The *Adamant* had been well stocked with food and drink, and all of the passengers (except, of course, those who were chained in the hold with Ethan Allen) had spent most of their trip reveling in the fine fare and in one another's company. Brant and Oteronyente probably wondered what delights lay in store for them in England after having such a grand time aboard ship.

The warriors soon found that they would not be disappointed. With Johnson, they set off immediately for London, where the acting superintendent requested audiences with government officials that he believed might be of use to him politically. Sir Guy had taken over his position after the death of his uncle Sir William Johnson, who had previously held the post, but no one in the English government had yet formally recognized Sir Guy as the new superintendent. He was convinced that he would be given the job officially once the right people in the English government had seen firsthand his friendly relationship with his Indian companions. The British government desperately wanted to maintain close ties with the Mohawks, who were the most powerful of the six tribes in the mighty Iroquois nation. If the skirmishes staged by rebel leaders such as Allen grew into a full-scale war in the colonies, the British would have to rely on their Iroquois allies for military assistance.

An engraving of London in the mid-18th century. Although Brant was reared as a Mohawk, his European-style education allowed him to hold his own among the many dignitaries he met in the cosmopolitan city.

Responses to Johnson's requests came quickly. The first invitation came from the king himself, who was eager to meet the two Indian warriors. On February 29, Johnson, Brant, and Oteronyente arrived at St. James's Palace for a dinner in their honor. The three men were graciously received by King George, Queen Charlotte, and their children and had a fine time at the feast that followed. Indeed, Brant was so impressed by George III that, years later, he maintained, "A finer man . . . I think it [would] be a truly difficult task to find."

Two weeks after their royal reception, the three men were granted an audience with Lord George Germain, the British secretary of colonial affairs. At this meeting, Brant set about the tasks that the leaders of the Mohawks had sent him across the ocean to perform. After a bit of small talk with Germain, the Indian ambassador got down to business. He first informed Germain that the British colonial subjects in New York were behaving very badly toward their Mohawk neighbors. They were making false claims on Indian land, hunting on tribal territory, and generally making a nuisance of themselves. He then reminded Germain of the years of faithful service that the Mohawks and the other Iroquois tribes had given to Great Britain:

> We have been often assured by our late great friend Sir William Johson who never deceived us, and we know he was told so that the King and wise men here would do us justice; but this notwithstanding all our applications has never been done, and it makes us very uneasie. Indeed it is very hard when we have let the Kings subjects have so much of our lands for so little value, they should want to cheat us in this manner of the small spots we have left for our women and children to live on. We are tired out in making complaints & getting no redress.

As many British officials had done before, Germain promised Brant that his grievances would be addressed once the troubles with the rebels were over. He also added shrewdly that the more military assistance the British received from the Indians, the sooner these problems were likely to end.

Johnson, Brant, and Oteronyente left Germain's office satisfied that they had accomplished their goals for the trip. Now they were free for more pleasurable activities, such as making names for themselves in the social circles of London. Their meeting with the king had given them an air of distinction that made them desirable dinner and party guests.

At one affair, held by the Earl of Warwick, Brant sat for a portrait. The earl had hired famed British artist George Romney to execute the work. In the painting, Brant appears as a pensive but elegant figure, dressed partly in Indian garb and partly in the fashionable clothing of a British aristocrat. His clothing and demeanor reveal Brant's connection with both of those worlds. Brant had been reared as a Mohawk but had received a European-style education at a school in Connecticut. The

This portrait, painted by English artist George Romney in 1776, greatly pleased Brant. He was only 33 when it was painted, but his expression and stance reveal his confidence in his role as a diplomat for the Iroquois nation.

knowledge of British speech and customs he acquired there had made him an excellent choice to represent the Mohawks in their dealings with the British government.

Despite all the hospitality offered them by British society, Brant and Oteronyente spent their most enjoyable days in London in the company of Gilbert Tice, an American innkeeper who was traveling in England. With him, the Mohawk men toured the sights of the city. (The Tower of London was their favorite.) The three also loved sharing stories around the table at the Swan with Two Necks Inn, where Brant and Oteronyente were staying. Indeed, the two Indians enjoyed the bustling life of the inn so much that when they were invited to move to more upscale lodgings, they flatly refused. With its constant influx of traders, traveling merchants, and other interesting clientele, the inn must have reminded the Mohawks of their home village of Canajoharie.

One of the social functions to which Gilbert Tice brought Brant and Oteronyente was a ball at Haber-dashers' Hall. Here the two Indians were introduced to many people in London's merchant class. They also met a young journalist employed by the *London Magazine* named James Boswell. (Boswell would later become well known in British literary history for his biography of writer Samuel Johnson.) Boswell found Brant extremely interesting and asked to interview him. The Mohawk agreed, and the two men met at the Swan with Two Necks several days later.

The article Boswell wrote about Brant reveals that the Englishman had not expected an Indian to be so well spoken or dressed in the latest English fashions. Boswell was also surprised when Brant informed him that he was hard at work on translating the New Testament into the Mohawk language. This endeavor was hardly what the British public had been led to believe would be of interest to an Indian. For years, reports from the colonies had been filled with tales of Indians' savagery and cruelty, leading most Englishmen to think of Indian people as little more than wild animals. Boswell seemed somewhat disappointed that Brant did not live up to these myths. He noted, almost forlornly, that his subject "had not the ferocious dignity of a savage leader."

As Brant's trip was drawing to a close, he took part in another activity unusual for an Indian. The Mohawk man was initiated into the Falcon Lodge of the Freemasons, an ancient fraternal organization to which many of the most influential men in Great Britain belonged. His sponsor was none other than George III. Brant would be the only Indian so honored for many, many decades.

On May 7, 1776, the great visit to London came to an end. Guy Johnson had received his commission as Indian superintendent to the colonies, and Joseph Brant and John Hill Oteronyente had presented their tribe's complaints to the proper authorities. The time had come to return to New York and aid in England's fight against the rebel forces.

The travelers set out for Falmouth, where they stocked up on last-minute supplies and gifts for their families before boarding the *Lord Hyde*, the ship that would take them to New York. They set sail in early June, as part of a huge fleet of ships that would carry men and supplies to the British forts and stockades in New York City and Albany. There were several gunboats with them, owing to the recent attacks on British ships by rebel sea forces, known as privateers.

As fate would have it, the *Lord Hyde* came under attack off the coast of Bermuda in mid-July. The ship was badly damaged but was able to defend itself successfully against capture. Reports from the crew indicate that, during the attack, Brant and Oteronyente made good use of firearms that they had purchased while in London.

King George III was so impressed by Brant that he sponsored the Mohawk for initiation into the Falcon Lodge of the Freemasons, an ancient fraternal organization to which many of the most influential men in Great Britain belonged.

The ship pulled into port at Staten Island on July 29, 1776. The two Indians were eager to begin their journey home. After all, they had not seen their families in almost a year and undoubtedly also wanted to pass on the good news of their meetings in England to the tribal leaders. However, Brant and Oteronyente soon discovered that while they were in England, many events had taken place that would alter their plans significantly. Perhaps the most important was the signing of the Declaration of Independence. There was now no question that the colonists and the British were at war and that the Iroquois' alliance with the British would bring unimagined and dramatic change to the world of the Mohawks. In this new world, young Joseph Brant would soon play one of the most crucial roles.

2

WARRIOR AND SCHOLAR

According to most scholars, Thayendanegea, who would later be known to the world as Joseph Brant, was born in March 1743 somewhere along the Cuyahoga River in present-day northeastern Ohio. His birthplace was far from the traditional Mohawk homeland in what is now east-central New York; however, it was common for Mohawk families to embark on lengthy trips to hunting grounds along the Cuyahoga and other Ohio River tributaries. For decades, the Indians had overhunted in their homeland, and as a result, there were few animals left there.

The Cuyahoga region was only a small part of the vast territories that had been taken over by the Iroquois, a confederacy of tribes that at its founding in the late 16th century included the Oneidas, the Onondagas, the Cayugas, the Senecas, and the Mohawks. During the early 17th century, the Iroquois had waged war to increase the amount of land they controlled by almost three times. This expansion gave the Iroquois enormous economic power, for they were able to acquire huge numbers of animal pelts by hunting on their new lands or by exacting tribute from the many tribes that they conquered in the Northeast, including the Mahicans, the Delawares, the Miamis, the Hurons, and the Potawatomis. These pelts

These drawings of Iroquois men and dwellings were made by Charles Bécard de Granville, a French official in Canada, in about 1700. They are among the earliest non-Indian representations of Indian peoples in the Northeast.

could then be traded to Europeans for manufactured goods—such as cloth, metal tools, guns, and ammunition—that were greatly desired by all Indians. As a result of the Iroquois' economic wealth and unrelenting ferocity in gaining and defending territory, they became so feared that no other Indian group in the area dared to challenge their supremacy. Another consequence was that representatives from France, England, and the Netherlands did everything they could to gain the Iroquois' support in their conquest of North America.

Of the scant information that exists about Joseph's family before his birth, most comes from a registry kept by an Anglican missionary named Henry Barclay, who lived near the Mohawk village of Canajoharie. According to the registry, Joseph's father was known as Peter Tehonwaghkwangeraghkwa (Peter being his baptized name). His mother was listed simply as Margaret, although she surely had a Mohawk name as well. The registry also records the 1735 baptism of a Mary Degonwadonti, the daughter of Margaret and an earlier husband. Mary Degonwadonti later became known as Molly Brant. The mission records indicate that Margaret gave birth to two children by Peter as well—a boy in 1741 and a girl in 1742. Both probably died in childhood. Sometime after the baptism of their second child, Peter and Margaret ceased to be mentioned in the registry. It was most likely at this time that they embarked on their journey to the western hunting territories where Joseph was born.

The registry also suggests that, although Joseph was destined to become a great leader and statesman, his beginnings were rather humble. Next to the name of each baptized child are the names of several members of his or her family who agreed to act as the child's sponsor. The sponsors listed for Peter and Margaret's children had no special social significance in their village, as they

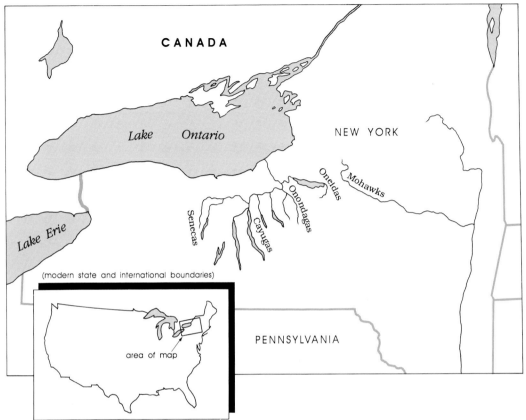

surely would have had, had Margaret been of high station. (Only Margaret's social standing would reflect on her children, because the Mohawks traced their ancestry through the mother's line—a practice known as matrilineality.)

It is known that Joseph was born into the Mohawks' Wolf clan, more evidence of his low social status. (Iroquois society was made up of many clans, each of which comprised a group of people who considered themselves closely related, shared property in common, and believed that they were descended from a common ancestor.) The Wolf clan had little impact on the governing of the Mohawks. Indeed, genealogical studies of Brant's ancestors have shown that although both his parents were full-fledged members of the Mohawk tribe, Brant was actually descended from Huron captives taken by the Mohawks during the Iroquois expansion. In Iroquois society, captives were usually adopted by the various tribes in order to make up for population losses resulting from disease and warfare.

Sometime in the 1740s, Joseph's father died, probably the victim of an epidemic that swept through the Ohio River valley and other nearby regions. Such outbreaks of disease were quite common among Indian populations that had come into contact with Europeans. Many diseases—including smallpox, influenza, and cholera— were introduced to North America by early European explorers, traders, and settlers. Because Indians had no natural immunities to these new illnesses, they readily caught them and died from them.

Without Peter to hunt for food, Margaret was forced to return to Canajoharie. There, she presumably moved in with some of her relatives and promptly had her unbaptized son christened Joseph. Like most Mohawks during this period, Margaret was a fairly dedicated Christian.

Mohawk tradition required tribe members to care for their impoverished relatives, but Margaret could not expect her family to feed her and her children forever. Overhunting had rendered food so scarce among the Mohawks that most Indians were living a hand-to-mouth existence by the time of Joseph's birth. As a result, they were growing increasingly unwilling to share what they had—even with family members.

The most convenient way for Margaret to remedy her situation was to remarry. Either in the hunting territory or back at Canajoharie, Margaret took a husband named Lykas in the late 1740s. Little is known of the couple's life other than that they settled in Canajoharie and had no recorded children. Margaret's reprieve from poverty did not last long, however. In May 1750, Lykas was killed by southern Indians during a war expedition.

Again, Margaret was left alone to provide for her children. It is unclear what course she took at that moment, but there were several options open to a woman of her low social status. One was to join the liquor trade by purchasing a large amount of alcohol and reselling it in small amounts to other Indians for a profit. Another was to gather ginseng roots and exchange them for food and goods at the trading posts and forts in the area. White traders had found a ready market for ginseng in the lucrative trading centers of China, whose citizens valued the root as a spice and health aid.

In any case, Margaret soon took the most obvious way out of her financial difficulties and married yet again. According to the journal of Reverend John Ogilvie, Margaret had caused a commotion among the inhabitants of Canajoharie by bearing the child of a village sachem, or elder, named Brant. (His Mohawk name was Canagaraduncka.) On March 4, 1753, Reverend Ogilvie baptized the child Jacob and recorded his name in the parish register. The following September, he officiated at and recorded the marriage of Margaret and Brant, an event that signaled a turn for the better in the lives of the unlucky Margaret and her children, Molly and Joseph.

Brant, as a sachem and member of the Mohawk leadership, was able to provide a very comfortable living for his new family members. He was a member of the influential Turtle clan and, as such, had connections with all of the other Iroquois leaders and the most important non-Indian traders and government officials in the area. Indeed, a 1755 document records that the governor of Pennsylvania himself presented Brant with a gift for Margaret when the sachem agreed to sign over some Iroquois land to the colony.

One influential man with whom Brant and the other Mohawk leaders had a great deal of contact was longtime trader Sir William Johnson. Johnson had come to the colony of New York from Ireland in 1738 to seek his fortune. A good talker and able trader, he quickly gained the confidence and the business of the Mohawks in the region. Within a few years of his arrival, Johnson had opened a trading post and general store on the bank of the Mohawk River opposite Canajoharie. Because of his fair prices and honest dealings with the Indians, he became very popular among them. He soon earned the Mohawk name Warraghiyagey (One Who Makes Much Business).

In 1755, Johnson was appointed superintendent of Indian affairs by the British government. This position had many responsibilities, including overseeing trade between Indians and the British and distributing presents to the Indians to maintain their loyalty to the Crown. One of Johnson's first acts in this new capacity was to call a meeting at his home, Johnson Hall, where he tried

A 1786 engraving of the battlefield at Lake George, where 250 Mohawk warriors joined 2,000 British troops to defeat a sizable French force in 1755. After this battle, the British assumed the Mohawks were their military allies and expected the Indians' assistance in many other conflicts during the French and Indian War.

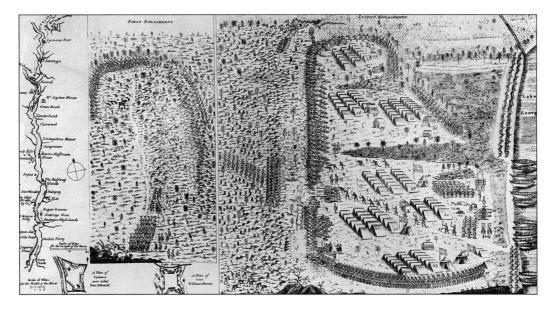

to convince many of the Iroquois to fight alongside the British against the French. The two nations were engaged in a battle for control over North America that would become known as the French and Indian War. Normally, the Iroquois tried to stay neutral in the conflicts that raged between Europeans, but they so trusted Johnson that they agreed to involve themselves in the war.

After winning the Indians over, Johnson quickly organized the Iroquois warriors. He then led an army of British and Iroquois troops in a victorious battle against the French at what is now the town of Lake George in east-central New York State. After this success, the Mohawks were considered British allies for the duration of the French and Indian War—a distinction that brought the tribe many more casualties than rewards.

In the summer of 1758, Johnson again led a force of some 400 Mohawks and other Indian warriors in a raid against the French stockade at Ticonderoga, which lay about 50 miles north of Lake George. This time, the Mohawk elders considered the 15-year-old Joseph mature enough to go into battle. The boy must have greatly looked forward to the adventure. When the fighting began, however, it was not excitement that gripped the young warrior—it was terror. A missionary recorded Joseph's feelings many years later: "[I] was seized with such [fear] when the firing began that [I] was obliged to take hold of a small sapling to steady [my]self." But Joseph soon recovered his composure and faced up to the bloody battle. If he had not, his career as a Mohawk leader would never have begun.

At Ticonderoga, Joseph was witness to a rousing British defeat. The Indian warriors stood back and watched in horror as more than 10,000 British troops were routed by a French army half their size. That the British continued to fight after losing many hundreds of men seemed unconscionable to the Mohawks. According to the Iroquois' war customs, a war party ceased fighting immediately upon the death of a warrior because a loss of even a single man was considered a great tragedy. Consequently, the Mohawks were disdainful of the actions of the British leaders at the battle. Historian Isabel Thompson Kelsay has noted that many Mohawk leaders mockingly called British general James Abercromby an "old Squaw" and said that his army had "fine limbs but no head."

Despite this defeat, the Mohawks again accompanied the British in battle later that summer. This time, they joined Colonel John Bradstreet's troops against the French stronghold of Fort Frontenac in the Canadian colony of Quebec. The British were victorious, and Joseph was there to join in the celebrating and looting that followed.

By the beginning of 1759, there lay only one major obstacle to a complete British victory in America—Fort Niagara. This French installation lay at the headwaters of the Niagara River, which runs between Lake Ontario and Lake Erie. The garrison guarded the most important route to the western trapping grounds and the villages of the French-allied Indians, such as the Huron.

In June, Johnson decided the time had come for an assault on the fort. He led the Mohawks, including Joseph, on an arduous 140-mile trek from Canajoharie to the mouth of the Niagara. They arrived on July 7 and immediately began their attack. The battle went poorly for the French from the start. On July 25, the fort fell, and with it went French control of the western fur trade.

By late 1760, Sir William Johnson was ready to embark on the final stage of the British takeover of Canada. He and his troops marched northward in the summer to fight for control of Montreal, which they gained on September 8, 1760, after convincing French-allied Indians to side with the British or at least to become neutral. The Indians

The front (left) and back of a medal presented by the British government to a Mohawk named Tankalkel for his participation in the Battle of Montreal. Joseph was among the 180 other warriors also so honored.

wisely realized that there was little point in continuing to support the French.

The French and Indian War would continue for three more years, but the conflict at Montreal would be the last battle Joseph would fight for some time. Like his fellow Mohawk warriors, he returned home with some souvenirs and, undoubtedly, a sense of pride in himself and his nation. The next year, this feeling was bolstered when he and some 180 other Mohawks received medals of honor from the British crown to commemorate their participation in the Battle of Montreal. Each medal bore the image of the city on one side and the name of the Mohawk recipient on the other.

Johnson had spent a great deal of time at the home of Joseph's stepfather throughout the late 1750s. The two men made plans for battles, organized meetings between the various Iroquois leaders, and probably engaged in quite a few purely social conversations. But there was still another reason for Johnson's frequent visits—his interest in Joseph's sister, Molly.

Molly was at least seven years older than her brother and was certainly of marriageable age at this time. In 1759, Johnson had lost his companion, Catharine Weissenberg, who, with her mother's help, had looked after his well-being at Johnson Hall. It is unclear whether Johnson and Weissenberg were ever legally married, but she definitely bore two children by him.

Either shortly before or soon after Weissenberg's death, Molly Brant took up residence at Johnson Hall. Although Johnson never married her, she was treated as his wife by the Iroquois and by much of the white population of the region. Johnson's importance and prominent position in the area protected him and Molly from any accusations of impropriety, even from the clergy.

This union had a very definite effect on Joseph's fortunes. In 1761, Johnson received a letter from a parson named Eleazar Wheelock, who ran a school for Indian boys in the town of Lebanon in Connecticut. In the letter, Wheelock informed Johnson that he had enough funds to support three new students and asked Johnson if he knew of any likely candidates.

Johnson thought immediately of his young friend and near-relative Joseph. The boy was intelligent, eager to learn, and had at least some knowledge of British customs. Johnson also suggested Sander and Nickus, two close friends of Joseph's. On August 1, 1761, the three young men arrived at Parson Wheelock's school, tired and hungry from their long ride on horseback. The new pupils were greeted with a bath and a set of European-style clothes.

The next day, they learned what life at the school would be like. At sunrise, they were called to a church service. They then had their morning meal in the school's communal dining hall, after which they were allowed an hour or so to themselves. After a brief prayer, the morning lessons began at nine o'clock sharp. The curriculum included many subjects, but reading, writing, and speaking English and training in European etiquette and Christian behavior were stressed. The boys also had lessons in Latin, Greek, Hebrew, and arts and sciences.

The three Mohawks soon became immersed in their lessons, but when in the fall the time came for a visit home, Sander and Nickus were eager to go. Both left for Canajoharie in September, neither to return. Not long after their arrival, Sander died, and Nickus married a young woman from the village and elected to settle there.

Joseph stayed on at the school until November. Unlike his friends, he had adapted well to his new environment. Wheelock's knowledge that the boy was a favorite of the influential Johnson may have caused the schoolmaster to treat Joseph better than the others.

When Brant finally left for his visit to Canajoharie, he was accompanied by Samuel Kirkland, one of the school's few white students. Kirkland had been charged with choosing two more prospective Mohawk pupils. When the two young men arrived in the village, Joseph found Canajoharie in turmoil. He learned an epidemic had swept through the settlement and killed many of its inhabitants, although all of Joseph's immediate family members had survived. He also soon discovered that a worse plague had begun to display its first symptoms— white encroachment onto Mohawk land. Several unfortunate events had resulted in the Mohawks' loss of large amounts of land to unscrupulous white speculators. In one such transaction, a white man named Phillip Livingston obtained a large portion of land on the eastern border of Canajoharie. Joseph found out that Livingston and his partners then made an illegal survey of the land, which they used to claim that the tract they obtained included the Indians' homes and fields.

Still another problem facing the residents of Canajoharie was caused by their British "allies." During the French and Indian War, the Iroquois had been promised free and easy trade with the British in return for aid to the British cause. After the war, however, trading had become much more difficult for the Indians. They were treated as beggars and thieves by the British at the military trading posts. Additionally, through long contact with non-Indian culture and its goods, the Mohawks had become completely dependent on European ammunition, cooking utensils, textiles, and other goods. Consequently, the Indians' very survival was threatened by any decrease in the flow of trade goods.

Because they were so favored by William Johnson, the Mohawks were probably less troubled by these trade difficulties than were the other Iroquois tribes. The situation was so bad for the Senecas, the westernmost Iroquois nation, that rumors began to fly that they were planning revenge against the British. The French traders of regions surrounding Lake Ontario and Lake Erie had been put out of business by the British and were therefore more than happy to feed the Indians' growing resentment toward their former allies. Indeed, the western Iroquois had sent messages to the Mohawks' leaders claiming that an army of combined French and Indian forces had taken British forts in the Ohio country and killed or captured many hundreds of men.

Joseph's visit lasted only two weeks, but the disturbing things he had learned and witnessed in Canajoharie surely kept his young mind distracted long after his return to Parson Wheelock's school. No matter how difficult it was to settle back down to his studies, chores, and prayers, Joseph was equal to the task—even able to relish it. He made incredible progress in mastering spoken and written English, which, for a native speaker of Mohawk, was extremely difficult.

At Parson Eleazar Wheelock's school for Indian boys, Joseph learned to read and write English and to conduct himself according to the rules of European etiquette. Wheelock was pleased with the progress of his student, whom he called, "a young Mohawk . . . of a Sprightly Genius, a manly and genteel Deportment, and of a Modest courteous and benevolent Temper."

Brant took to his religious studies just as actively. Parson Wheelock was a devout Christian and a rousing speaker, and he apparently passed his religious fervor on to his young Mohawk student. When writing of his students to a friend, he singled out Joseph as an example of success:

> A young Mohawk . . . of a Sprightly Genius, a manly and genteel Deportment, and of a Modest courteous and benevolent Temper, I have Reason to think [he] began truly to love our Lord Jesus Christ Several Months ago; and his religious Affections Seem Still agre[e]ably increasing.

By the spring of 1763, Joseph was well on his way to becoming a religious scholar. As such, the most logical career for him was to serve as a Christian missionary to his people. Joseph was presented with just such an opportunity when his classmate Charles Jeffry Smith proposed that Joseph accompany him to the Oneida village of Oquaga. There Smith planned to found a mission and wanted Joseph to act as his interpreter.

Wheelock was equally excited by the prospect. He quickly sent off a letter to Johnson in order to gain his approval. While Joseph prepared to leave, a response arrived. However, the letter was from Joseph's sister, Molly, not Johnson. She told Joseph to forget about his missionary activities and return immediately to Canajoharie. She offered no explanations, but Joseph had no choice but to obey. On July 5, he and Smith started out for the Mohawk village. Neither man had any idea that Joseph's life as a missionary was about to end before it began.

*An Indian council at Johnson
Hall, the house of British superintendent of Indian affairs Sir
William Johnson. The leaders
of the Mohawks considered
Johnson a great friend and
often gathered at his home to
ask his advice on how best to
express their desires and
grievances to the British crown.*

3

A NEW BEGINNING

Even after leaving Parson Wheelock's school, Brant and Smith held on to their dream of establishing a mission. The first stop they made on their trip was a supply store in Albany, where they purchased the goods that they would need for their work among the Oneidas. From the store's owner, however, they received news that could only mean they would have to put their own plans on hold.

Two months earlier, an Ottawa Indian leader named Pontiac had attacked a British fort at Detroit. Pontiac's forces (made up of Ottawa, Huron, Potawatomi, and Chippewa warriors) were unable to penetrate the defenses of the fort, so they dug in for a siege. Not long after this attack, several other forts and stockades in the eastern Great Lakes region fell to Indian raiders, including Fort Venango, which was taken by Seneca forces from the village of Geneseo. When word of these attacks reached Johnson Hall, William Johnson busied himself with recruiting an army of settlers to guard New York in case Pontiac's forces moved eastward.

The settlers' preparations for battle must have impressed Brant and Smith as they continued their journey. They traveled quickly, heading for Johnson Hall, where they hoped to get advice from Sir William. Much to their alarm and disappointment, he told them that under no circumstances should they continue on to Oquaga. Johnson urged them to remain in Canajoharie, where they would be safe from attack, and to attend a conference that he had arranged with the leaders of the Iroquois. The two men agreed and settled in at Margaret's home.

When the conference convened, tempers were high among all the participants. Johnson was especially perturbed that no representatives of the Seneca nation had chosen to attend. Although the Seneca leaders had not condoned the actions of the Geneseo villagers who had assisted the warring western tribes, their absence from the conference suggested that they did not condemn them, either. The Iroquois leaders who were present promised to send a delegation to reprimand the Senecas, for they believed, and probably rightly so, that their nations could not afford to antagonize the British.

The delegation tried to persuade the Senecas to recall their warriors, but to no avail. In the months that followed the conference, the fighting escalated at an alarming rate. The inhabitants of Detroit were still imprisoned in their own homes by Pontiac's forces. The few attempts to break the siege had resulted in the death of many British soldiers. And to the east and south, the Delawares and Geneseo Senecas continued to attack settlers and military personnel, killing hundreds and capturing hundreds more.

On October 7, 1763, King George III finally took action to stop the bloodshed. For some time, he and his advisers had been trying to come up with a plan that would both appease the Indians and keep the non-Indian immigrants from aggressively taking over Indian land. The settlers saw the vast empty spaces of the tribal territories as good farmland that was going to waste. They did not understand that the Indians hunted and gathered a great deal of their food and needed large tracts to support their small tribal populations.

William Johnson regarded the young Brant almost as a son. Largely owing to Johnson's influence, Brant was slowly able to move into a position of leadership among the Iroquois.

The king's answer to these problems was the Proclamation of 1763. This edict established a boundary between Indian country and colonial territory. The border ran down the length of the Appalachian Mountains. The land to the east was reserved for white settlement, and the land to the west was designated as Indian property.

For Brant, this must have been a very uneasy time. He was unable to continue with his plans for a missionary life, and because he had spent so much time away from Canajoharie, he did not really have a place in the activities of his village, either. Once again, his father and Johnson were able to use their influence to help him. On several occasions, the Mohawk leaders appointed young Brant to carry messages to Johnson Hall, an honor usually reserved for men from more powerful clans, in preparation for a new council to be held in the late summer.

When the council convened, representatives from the Oneidas, Onondagas, Cayugas, Mohawks, and Tuscaroras (who had joined the Iroquois Confederacy in 1722) were present. This time, leaders from two of the three major Seneca towns were also in attendance, which soothed some tension. Yet with all the disagreements among the tribes, little was accomplished.

The council was a success in one respect, however. Johnson was able to obtain enough information to form a plan for getting control of the situation in the west. A delegation of Caughnawaga Indians from Canada had attended the meeting and offered to send a war party against the rebel Indian forces. Johnson liked the idea and by early 1764 had overcome the initial opposition of the Iroquois and the British military.

He then asked the Iroquois to provide warriors for the expedition. Most of the volunteers were Mohawks and Oneidas. These tribes lived farthest from the fighting in the west and therefore, perhaps, were less sympathetic to the plight of the Delaware, Shawnee, and western Seneca peoples.

The British and Mohawk forces, which included Brant, set off for Oquaga on February 9, 1764, where they planned to collect their Oneida allies. The war party arrived in the village in late February, but owing to the Oquaga warriors' lengthy war preparations, it was not able to set off for battle until late March. During the delay, Brant got to meet with the people whose souls he had planned to save. He found, however, that the village already had a very strong religious leader, a man named Isaac. Brant apparently got along well with Isaac, because the leader introduced the young man to his family.

When it finally got off the ground, the war expedition was a success. After a few weeks of raiding enemy towns, destroying livestock and homes, and carrying away provisions, the troops turned back. Brant, who spent much of the campaign ferrying reports to Johnson, returned to Canajoharie on April 20, 1764.

With the troubles to the west resolved for the time being, life in Canajoharie settled back to its normal routine. During the next year, Brant took advantage of this period of relative peace and traveled back and forth to Oquaga several times. Brant made these journeys in order to court Peggie, the daughter of Isaac. The court-ship went well, and on July 22, 1765, Joseph and Peggie were married. Anglican minister Theophilus Chamber-lain performed the British-style ceremony and described Peggie as "handsome, Sober, discreet & a religious young woman."

After the wedding, Brant moved his new wife into his mother's home at Canajoharie. This arrangement went against Mohawk custom, by which a man usually resided in the home of his wife's parents. Possibly, Brant had become so important to his community that he felt required to live there.

Brant's inclusion in a delegation of Mohawk leaders that met with Johnson in early winter of 1765 was evidence of his growing influence. Few men of Brant's age would have been allowed to accompany the important leaders of the delegation, but they recognized that, as a sort of relative of Sir William's, he might help persuade Johnson to hear them out. The leaders asked for an update on what the Crown was doing about their troubles with whites encroaching on their land and requested the services of a blacksmith. Johnson responded that the king was working to resolve both problems.

The following spring, Brant joined another delegation, this one organized by Johnson. Before traveling to a peace treaty council with Pontiac and the other western Indians that was to be held at Fort Ontario, Johnson arranged for several prominent Mohawks, including Joseph and Peggie, to accompany him.

Largely through Johnson's influence, Brant was given a position as an interpreter at the fort. His duties included acting as a go-between for white and Indian traders and as a spokesman at the many conferences that took place between the local Indian leaders and the fort's commanding officers. The work was not difficult, and Brant was paid £70 a week, a handsome sum.

Nevertheless, Brant was not happy in his job. Less than two months after taking the position, he began asking Sir William to transfer him back home. Brant's unhappiness may have stemmed from the commanding officer's mandate that he live in the soldier's barracks rather than with his wife. After the birth of the couple's first child, a son named Karaguantier and later christened Isaac after Peggie's father, Brant's complaints grew more urgent and more frequent. He was finally allowed to leave, and by early March 1676, the Brant family was back in Canajoharie.

Once he was settled again in Margaret's home, Brant

A medal given by Sir William to the western Iroquois at the Fort Ontario peace treaty council of 1766. The medal bears the words "Happy While United" and the image of an Indian and an Englishman shaking hands while sharing a peace pipe.

set about making a living. He earned money by interpreting for Johnson and the other British officials, by running a small mercantile shop, and perhaps by working as a longshoreman at the village canals. He seems to have done very well at all of these enterprises. His house was well stocked with food, furniture, and luxury goods; he and his wife were always well dressed; and he had credit lines with all of the major stores in the region. Brant also was very generous with his wealth. He had dozens of visitors between 1765 and 1768, most of whom were missionaries and students at Wheelock's school. All were well fed and well rested when they left Brant's home.

Although much of Brant's time was spent either making money or entertaining visitors, he was still able to attend to tribal affairs. He spoke many times with Johnson about issues that were troubling the Mohawks, including an incident in which a white land speculator named Cobus Maybe generously supplied some warriors with liquor and then kidnapped three of them. Maybe planned to take the men to Albany and, once there, compel them to sign over a large tract of Mohawk land. Luckily, Brant and an important Mohawk leader discovered the plan and intercepted the group before it reached Albany.

Land disputes continued to be a problem throughout Iroquois territory, and Johnson knew that some official action was needed to put a halt to them. Inspired by the success of the Proclamation of 1763, he proposed that a boundary be drawn between Iroquois territory and the lands of British settlers. After some hesitation, the Crown agreed to the plan, and arrangements for negotiating the placement of the boundary began. Johnson sent messages (many surely carried by Brant) to every Iroquois leader, asking them to come to a meeting at centrally located Fort Stanwix.

A document signed by the leaders of the Iroquois acknowledging their receipt of money in exchange for lands ceded in the 1768 Treaty of Fort Stanwix. Brant's signature (the fourth from the top in the second column) reads "Joseph Thayendanegea," a combination of his baptismal name and the Mohawk name he was given at birth. The drawing beside his signature indicates his membership in the Wolf clan.

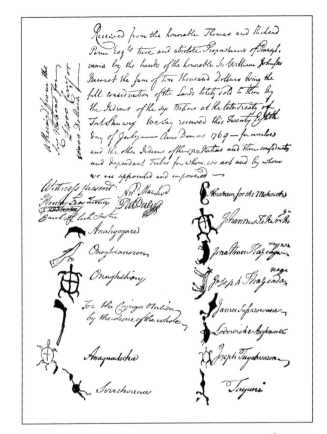

The negotiations began on October 24, 1768, and were attended by thousands of Indians representing tribes from Canada to Virginia. All of these tribes had an interest in the proceedings, for the Iroquois planned to cede land that included many of their homelands—tracts in what are today the states of Tennessee, Kentucky, West Virginia, Pennsylvania, and New York.

After 13 days, the meetings concluded with the signing of a treaty in which the Iroquois passed a huge amount of land into British hands. The value of the Treaty of Fort Stanwix to the Iroquois was readily apparent. A pile of the goods and cash, worth some $50,000, granted to them by the treaty was spread out for all to see in the fort's central square. The leaders divided the spoils among their people, and then the whole assembly set off for the long trip back home.

For the British, the success of the treaty was somewhat more questionable. The Iroquois' claim to many of the landholdings they had ceded was unsubstantiated. True, they had conquered almost all of the tribes in the territories in question, but most of the conquests had taken place more than 100 years earlier. Therefore, the British feared that the tribes in the ceded areas would make counterclaims for their homelands. The king understandably accepted the news of the treaty with some misgivings.

After the close of the negotiations, Brant returned home, probably a bit richer, but perhaps also a bit more worried. The Mohawk villages of Canajoharie and Fort Hunter now existed as virtual islands in a sea of white settlers because they were located on the British side of the new boundary line.

Despite these concerns, Brant settled back into his usual everyday activities. He continued to find innovative ways to make a good living, and Peggie gave birth to a second child, Christina. However, these prosperous and happy times for the Brant family soon ended when Peggie contracted tuberculosis and died in the spring of 1771.

Little is known of Brant's actions immediately after the death of his wife. He probably spent a great deal of time with clergymen. By the following spring, he was hard at work assisting John Stuart—the missionary appointed to the church at Fort Hunter—in translating the church service into the Mohawk language. The two men went on to translate the entire Gospel of Mark into Mohawk.

Unfortunately, these friends eventually had a falling out over a certain Mohawk tradition. According to tribal custom, when a man lost his wife, her family was bound to provide him with another. In the late winter of 1773,

Brant asked Stuart to marry him to Peggie's half sister Susanna. Not understanding or respecting Mohawk ways, the clergyman refused, declaring that such a union was improper. Despite Stuart's objections, Joseph and Susanna were soon wed.

Brant continued to prosper at Canajoharie, although renewed troubles on the western frontier began to prey on his mind and those of his fellow Mohawks. Just as the British had feared, the western tribes were beginning to wake up to the injustices that had been inflicted on them by the Treaty of Fort Stanwix. The Shawnees and Delawares had again begun to raid white villages and kill their inhabitants. Troops from those colonies neighboring Indian country retaliated in an equally bloody manner. Once again, the threat of war hovered over the Iroquois nations, and once again they appealed to Johnson for help.

On July 9, 1774, a group of Iroquois leaders met at Johnson Hall and voiced their concerns to Sir William. They complained of the continual encroachment of white settlers on Iroquois territory. For two days, Johnson listened and responded. At about 6:00 P.M. on July 11, he retired to his home, and the Indians settled down for a long night's debate over Johnson's statements. They planned to discuss their conclusions with him in the morning, fully expecting to be able to resolve their grievances with him, as they had so many times in the past.

But two hours later, they learned that this meeting would have an unexpected ending. A British spokesman came to the assembled Indians and informed them that Johnson had just died. Shocked by the news, the saddened Iroquois slowly realized that they had lost more than a great friend and trusted adviser. With Johnson's passing, their close ties to the British government were likely to be severed forever.

4

TORIES AND REBELS

A portrait of Guy Johnson, painted by the American artist Benjamin West in London in 1776. The shadowed Indian warrior in the background suggests Sir Guy's recent appointment as superintendent of Indian affairs. Johnson's dress, which includes a hat, sash, and shoes adorned with Indian beadwork, is typical of the clothing worn by officials of the British Indian department.

For Joseph Brant and his family, the death of Sir William brought some significant changes. His sister, Molly, and eight of her children moved back to Canajoharie, leaving Johnson Hall to the other children of her former companion. Molly did not, however, leave empty-handed. She returned to her home village with several servants, 500 pieces of silver jewelry, 12 chairs, a boat, and a white formal gown. She owned several homes in the village and probably moved into one of them.

With Johnson's passing, Brant had lost both a good friend and an employer. However, Guy Johnson, Sir William's nephew, took over his uncle's official duties and soon assured Brant that his service with the Indian department (the part of the British government charged with dealing with England's Indian allies) would continue. In fact, Brant's responsibilities increased. Previously, he had served as one of many interpreters and messengers. Now Brant was in charge of interpreting at all treaty negotiations and other Indian councils.

At that time, relations between the British and the Iroquois were generally calm. However, the troubles between the British and their colonial subjects were deepening at an alarming rate. The Iroquois' leaders heard many rumors of these problems and came to Guy

Park, Johnson's home, to ask him about one in particular. The Indians had seen a great number of British troops heading toward Boston and wondered why. From Johnson, they learned of the Boston Tea Party, an incident in which a group of colonists sneaked onto a ship belonging to a British tea merchant and threw its cargo overboard. The colonists were protesting a harsh tax on tea that the British crown had imposed.

Guy Johnson was a loyal British subject, or Tory, as they came to be called by the colonists. He thought that such incidents were the acts of troublemakers and scofflaws and assured the Iroquois that the British government would put a stop to them. The tribal leaders accepted this explanation and headed home.

For all their efforts, however, the British were having an extremely difficult time controlling the angry colonists. Throughout the 13 colonies and other British territories, people were taking up arms. Guy Johnson himself began to hear rumors that made him fear for his safety. One came from a British spy in Philadelphia who informed Johnson that he had heard of rebel plans to arrest Johnson and his staff. Johnson immediately stepped up security around his home and had Brant draft a letter to the Oneidas asking for military aid. Unfortunately, the letter went astray and was confiscated by local rebel leaders. The contents of the letter were in no way threatening to the rebels, but they were interpreted as such. Anti-British settlers were constantly afraid of a Johnson-inspired Indian attack. As a result, their leaders sent a deputation to meet with Johnson and the Indian leaders. Both sides promised to maintain the peace, and each also remained skeptical that the other's promises would be kept.

In early May 1775, conditions were still tense. Johnson, Brant, and several other Indian department employees decided to hold council at the village of Onondaga. Before leaving, Johnson received a message through secret channels from General Thomas Gage, the head of the British military in North America. It instructed Johnson to gather his most loyal associates, both Indian and white, and come quickly to Montreal. There they would join a force that would march under General Guy Carleton against the rebels of the New England colonies.

Johnson could not have been happier about the orders. He was now freed from both the threat of arrest by the rebels and his increasing troubles with the Indians. He immediately prepared to depart for Canada, as did many of his employees and constituents, including Brant.

The journey took the party through the territory of all the Iroquois nations. At each village, Johnson begged the leaders to allow their warriors to join his troops. But in every town, he was met with polite refusals. The Indians offered their loyalty to the king, but they were not willing to send their warriors to die for him. In fact, their arguments were so persuasive that many of the Mohawks in the war party decided to go back home.

When the group arrived in Montreal, they found themselves in the midst of yet another council. This one was between the British military and the Canadian Indians. General Carleton exhorted the Indians to fight in the service of the king. However, he then said the Indians could fight only within the borders of Quebec province. Guy Johnson was outraged, as Brant and the other Indians must have been. After all, the Indians considered themselves members of sovereign nations, not British subjects to be ordered around.

During the battle, the Indian warriors distinguished themselves, even on their restricted field. The deputy superintendent of Indian affairs in Canada, Daniel Claus, reported that Brant had fulfilled his duties to the utmost. But Brant's nephew, Peter Johnson, had perhaps the finest moment, one that provided General Carleton with something of a slap in the face. The 16-year-old Peter was among the British unit that surrounded famed rebel leader Ethan Allen. Allen, finding himself outnumbered, decided to surrender to the officer with the most noble appearance and picked the young Mohawk, whose demeanor clearly reflected his gentlemanly upbringing at Johnson Hall.

By the middle of August, the rebel forces were all but routed, and many of the Indian troops headed homeward. Guy Johnson then turned his attention to a more personal problem—convincing the Crown to formally name him his uncle's successor as the superintendent of Indian affairs. He decided to go to England and make a personal application to the colonial secretary. The few Mohawk leaders remaining with him elected to send their own deputation along on the trip. They told Brant and John Hill Oteronyente to act as their emissaries to George III, and then they headed for home.

When the three men boarded a ship for England in New York, the British were still firmly in control of the city. When they returned in July 1776, almost a year later, the situation had changed. The British still controlled Staten Island and some portions of Long Island, but they had lost Manhattan to the rebels.

Brant stayed in New York, resting from his long journey, until the fall. As winter approached, the warfare slowed to a standstill, and he took this opportunity to make the trip home in relative safety. He was eager to see his family and to tell the leaders the results of his mission to Great Britain.

With his traveling companion, Gilbert Tice, he arrived in Oquaga, where his family was now living, about four weeks later. Brant passed out to his friends and family the gifts that he had purchased in England, told the village leaders the tale of his journey, and encouraged them to pledge their military support to Britain. The two men then sent messages to Canajoharie and Fort Hunter asking the Mohawk warriors to meet them at Fort Niagara, where Brant hoped to get further instructions from its commander, John Butler. On the way to Niagara, Brant and Tice stopped at many Iroquois villages and repeated their tales and messages. They heard many promises to help the British, but most would turn out to be empty.

Brant was in good spirits when he reached Niagara, but they were quickly dashed. Butler refused to allow Brant to hold his meeting with the Mohawks there. It seemed he shared General Carleton's prejudice against Indian participation in battle. Brant quickly left the fort and again traveled through all the Iroquois villages. But again his efforts were inconclusive.

A request for supplies sent from Brant to a British official in July 1777. Brant's formation of his own army—known as Brant's Volunteers—initially received more support from local English settlers than from the British government.

In the spring of 1777, Brant returned to his friends and relatives at Oquaga bitterly disappointed with the poor results of his mission. He set about planning new strategies and waiting for orders from the British military. Not long after he arrived, white strangers began to arrive in the village, seeking to join forces with Brant. The upbringing and connections that made Brant seem an upstart to some of the older Iroquois made him a very appealing leader to the desperate pro-British settlers in the region. Within a few months, Brant had a force of more than 100 men, white and Indian, under his command.

Brant's Volunteers, as they became known, soon received orders from General Carleton, who had finally received enough pressure from the British government to allow the Indians to join in the fighting. The soldiers were instructed to make for the fort at Oswego, where they would join British forces led by General Barry St. Leger. The plan was to then retake Fort Stanwix, which had been captured by the rebels.

When they arrived at Fort Stanwix, the troops were confident about their mission and hoped to get it over with quickly. The rebels were greatly outnumbered and undersupplied. St. Leger was convinced that his men would merely have to sit outside the fort for a few days and the rebels would be frightened into surrendering. He was mistaken. Two days after the siege began, Brant received word from his sister, Molly, at Canajoharie. She warned him that rebel general Nicholas Herkimer was bringing a large party of reinforcements to the fort.

As it turned out, the rebels found another strategy to fend off St. Leger's troops, one that allowed them to keep Fort Stanwix without engaging in battle. Rebel general George Schuyler sent a spy into St. Leger's camp who pretended to have just escaped from a huge force of rebels and displayed clothing covered with bullet holes as evidence. This ruse may or may not have convinced the British, but it had its intended effect on the Indians—almost all of them fled. St. Leger then had no choice but to abandon the siege and head back to Oswego.

With winter setting in, all that Joseph Brant and the other military leaders—British, rebel, and Indian alike—could do was plan for the next spring. Joseph headed for Fort Niagara and spent those long, cold months developing strategies with the Seneca chief Sayengaraghta.

When spring arrived, Brant and his men were one of the first groups to set out. They immediately launched attacks on several rebel outposts and the towns that surrounded them. These raids were successful, but Brant was faced with several serious problems. His troops had little food. Even well-connected generals at Niagara, Detroit, and Montreal were hard-pressed to get supplies, so Brant's hopes of receiving goods from the British were slim. Brant was also concerned about his wife, Susanna, who had become ill during the summer. She died sometime that fall, a victim, like her half sister Peggie, of tuberculosis.

Adding to his problems was Walter Butler, the 25-year-old son of John Butler of Fort Niagara. The younger Butler was in charge of reinforcements sent to meet up with Brant's men in October. He had virtually no real combat experience, having spent most of the war thus far in a rebel prison in Albany.

Together the two leaders plotted an attack on the thriving town of Cherry Valley in present-day east-central New York. Brant and Butler instructed their men to destroy the town, take prisoners, and carry off whatever supplies they could. Because the force contained a large party of vengeful Seneca warriors who wanted to make the settlers pay for the lives of warriors lost in previous

battles, the leaders planned to get to the town ahead of their troops in order to oversee the attack. Unfortunately, the Senecas reached Cherry Valley first.

Things soon got out of hand. Most of the men and at least 30 women and children in the town were killed, scalped, and mutilated. The town was then put to the torch, and storehouses were looted. According to one rebel soldier, when Brant saw what had been done, he "turned round & wept and then recovering himself told Butler he was going to make war against America but not to Murder and Butcher."

News of the massacre at Cherry Valley spread like wildfire through rebel towns and encampments. Convinced they could not defend themselves against Indian

A painting of a 1778 battle in which British and Indian troops led by John Butler slaughtered 232 rebels living in the Wyoming valley of present-day eastern New York State. Although Brant was not present, rebel newspapers declared that he was responsible for the massacre. The menacing Indian figure in the foreground may be meant to represent Brant.

warfare, settlers fled by the hundreds from New York to safer quarters to the south. Meanwhile, rebel military leaders searched for strategies for fighting the "bloodthirsty savages."

After the destruction of Cherry Valley, the British forces again retired to Fort Niagara for the winter. In February 1779, Brant left these safe quarters for a brief trip to Quebec. There he met with the British commander, General Frederick Haldimand, and convinced the general to put him on the payroll of the Indian department.

When Brant returned to Niagara, he heard many confusing rumors. Some spies had been bringing back reports that the rebels were increasing their military activity. Others maintained the rebel leaders were growing desperate. General George Washington went so far as to write that "to defend an extensive frontier against the incursions of Indians and the Banditti under Butler and Brant is next to impossible."

Washington and his advisers came to the conclusion that their only hope of victory lay in the complete destruction of the Iroquois. In April 1779, Washington's troops set out for Onondaga, the heart of the Iroquois Confederacy. This town had been the site of all Iroquois councils for longer than even the oldest tribe member could remember. In the village square lay the council fire that, according to tradition, had burned continuously since the confederacy's creation more than 150 years earlier. When the rebel army attacked and destroyed the village, and extinguished the sacred fire, it did much more than wreck a few houses and cornfields—it shook the very foundations of the Iroquois world.

Brant and the British military leaders were thrown into turmoil. The British could not believe that the rebels had struck so deep into Iroquois territory without their gaining so much as a hint of the plan. Fort Niagara's commanding officer, Colonel Mason Bolton, immediately sent out several parties of troops, including one headed by Brant, to seek out information about the rebels' next moves. Brant first headed out westward toward Fort Detroit, but he learned of a rumored attack on Cayuga and turned toward that village instead. The rumor was untrue, so he and his Volunteers made for the village of Canadesaga (now Geneva) in order to meet up with Colonel John Butler's forces there. He and his men arrived in late June.

During the next two months, Brant and his men raided rebel towns and gathered supplies. Despite their successes, Brant became worried. The rebel militia was growing larger and more powerful. He alerted the British military commanders in Canada and northern New York that a full-scale rebel invasion of Iroquois country might be imminent. The generals thought such fears were groundless and made a few empty promises to send some more troops.

Unfortunately for the British, Brant was correct. For months, Washington had been readying for this great offensive. He entrusted its execution to three of his most capable officers—generals John Sullivan and James Clinton and Colonel Daniel Brodhead. With their armies positioned to the south, east, and west of Iroquois country, they struck at the end of July, burning every outlying Indian village that they came upon. Fields of ripening corn, beans, and squash went up in flames, as did homes, clothing, and all other possessions that the inhabitants had left behind when they fled. Brant and the two Butlers frantically tried to gather Indian and British forces to meet Clinton and Sullivan's combined forces. They attacked the rebel army near Newtown (now Elmira), but infighting and resentment between the

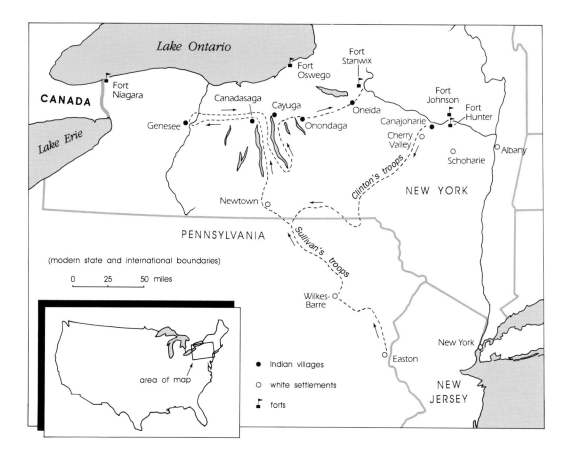

British and Indian troops turned the ambush into a retreat.

The rebels' advance continued. After sending several frantic pleas to Bolton at Niagara for reinforcements, Butler gathered his force of 400 men and prepared another ambush. When a rebel scouting party of about 30 men came into sight, the Indians in Butler's force impatiently attacked. During the brief battle, more than half of the rebels were killed, and four were taken prisoner, including two Indian guides.

When the main force of the rebel army, led by Clinton and Sullivan, reached the ambush spot, they found a hideous greeting. The two captured rebel soldiers had been tied to trees and beaten and tortured so badly that they were almost unrecognizable. (One soldier had been decapitated and his partially skinned head placed on a log.) The two generals were so horrified by this display that they turned homeward.

Brant and his men did their best to stay one step behind the rebel army. After the battle at Newtown, Brant had decided that if he could not defeat the rebels in battle, at least he could make a nuisance of himself and learn of any further plans through spying. He and his men took shots at the soldiers, worried their horses, and generally made it difficult for them to get a single night's sleep. Brant stayed so close that, as he explained many years later, he "roasted [his] venison by the fires that [the rebels] left behind."

By the time the rebels' trail of destruction had ended, cold weather forced Brant and his men to retire once again to Fort Niagara. Conditions at the fort were terrible. Hundreds of Iroquois refugees whose homes and food had been burned by the rebel army poured into the surrounding countryside, desperate for aid. But as always the supplies at Niagara were minimal. Aside from half-rotten fish heads and insect-infested bread, many refugees were left with nothing to eat but their own hide blankets.

Even during that harsh winter, there were some bright moments for Brant. In late 1779, he married for the third time. His new wife, Catharine Croghan, was the daughter of the head woman of the Mohawks. Catharine was next in line for that honored position and would have the right to choose the next chief, or Tekarihoga, for the tribe. Her power added greatly to Brant's own influence among the Iroquois.

Soon after the wedding, the couple moved into their own home on a piece of property upriver from the fort that Brant had bought several months earlier. Apparently

Brant had profited substantially from his stint as a British military leader. A historian named Isaac Weld, who visited Brant's new house, noted that he had several slaves in his service.

On February 8, 1780, Brant and his Indian warriors left their winter retreat and held a war dance at the home of Guy Johnson at Niagara in preparation for a raiding expedition. They captured a small group of rebel soldiers, but Brant decided to turn back to Niagara. His men were too ill and hungry to fight.

Back at the fort, Brant found two pleasant surprises waiting for him. The first was an official commission as a captain in the British Indian department, signed by General Haldimand. The second was an appointment to lead a division of Indian inhabitants of the fort. Guy Johnson had decided to place the Indians under the command of seven of his most trusted officers; Brant was the only Indian among them. Johnson instructed Brant to encourage the Indians to return to any lands that were still usable and get to work growing food.

By early July, Brant was ready to return to war. First, his troops made a surprise attack on the treacherous Oneidas, who continually spied for the rebel army and had taken part even in battles against their Iroquois compatriots. Next, they made a sweep through the settlements along the Mohawk River, destroying a large number of white settlements there, and joined a British force in attacking forts at the village of Schoharie. When Brant's troops returned to Niagara in late November, they felt that they had avenged themselves for the destruction of the Iroquois homeland.

The following spring, however, found the spirits of the British and their allies sinking lower and lower. They continued to attack rebel forts and settlements, but somehow the rebels always managed to find enough supplies to hold on. The continued pressures of war made even Brant lose control for a moment. After drinking heavily (unusual behavior for Brant), he became involved in a fight with one of his fellow officers. Rumors flew through the camp about the incident, but in the end the matter was resolved peaceably, and both men apologized.

In order to alleviate the situation, Guy Johnson decided to send Brant to Detroit in early April of 1781. At the large and bustling settlement, Brant attended a few councils and made some new friends. However, his thirst for vengeance soon overcame his sociability. He made his way to the town of Upper Sandusky, located approximately 150 miles south of Detroit in present-day Ohio, and quickly joined forces with an interpreter from the British Indian department named Simon Girty. Girty was making plans for a strike against rebel leader George Rogers Clark.

After two months of preparation, Girty's force was ready to move. Brant, with Girty's brother George, took a small party of Indian and white troops down the Ohio River. One night, Clark's large force passed the band, but Brant decided that their numbers were too small to initiate a confrontation with the rebels.

However, they did not leave the scene without a victory. Several days later, Brant's troops came upon a party of rebel soldiers led by Colonel Archibald Lochry who were trying to catch up with Clark. The Volunteers ambushed the rebels, killing 36 men, including Lochry, and taking the rest prisoner. Brant's soldiers got away without so much as a scratch. They sent their prisoners north to Detroit and, with the addition of a party of troops under Captain Alexander McKee, set off after Clark. But after hearing from several Indian scouts that Clark had decided to end his campaign for the remainder of the year, Brant and McKee chose not to risk losing their men

Captain Alexander McKee, Guy Johnson's deputy in Detroit, led a party of troops that joined with Brant's Volunteers to pursue George Rogers Clark's American force.

in what could have been a lopsided battle.

On their return journey to Detroit, relations between the Tory leaders turned unpleasant. The worst incident involved Brant and Simon Girty. While drinking, Brant bragged that he had bested most of Lochry's party by himself. Girty called him a liar, and Brant struck Girty in the forehead with his sword, causing a serious but not fatal wound. Brant himself received a leg injury, which either was inflicted by Girty or resulted from Brant's mishandling of his own sword.

Brant spent the rest of the year confined to bed, waiting for his wound to heal. He used his convalescence to plan the next spring's campaigns and meet with the leaders of western tribes. On one occasion, he spoke with several Huron and Shawnee chiefs about a possible attack on rebel-controlled Fort Pitt. However, Brant's plans were vetoed by General Haldimand, who realized that Pitt would be even more difficult to supply and defend than Niagara and Detroit.

By February 1782, Brant was well enough to attend the Indian councils that were in session at Detroit. At his first council, he made a speech in which he reaffirmed the Iroquois' devotion to the British cause and again warned Indians who sympathized with the rebels not to switch their loyalty:

> We invite you Brethren . . . to attend to what your father
> [General Haldimand] has said and not listen any more to
> the Rebels, lest that we who have not too much sense may
> fall out with each other should we not think with our
> father.

(These final words most likely were a sarcastic jab at the general's refusal to go along with Brant's Fort Pitt plan.)

At about the same time that this council was held, General Haldimand began hearing rumors that General Charles Cornwallis's troops were doing badly against the rebel forces of Pennsylvania. Indeed, several of the rumors hinted that Cornwallis had surrendered. If this were the case, then the rebel army would surely be heading north. Haldimand immediately began making plans to shore up and repair the fortifications at Oswego, which was the first point of defense on the fur-trade route. Haldimand also fired off a letter to the commander at Niagara asking him to recall Joseph Brant, who Haldimand considered to be "very usefull on this Occasion."

At Niagara, Brant learned that Cornwallis had indeed surrendered. Gathering his warriors and Volunteers, he then set off immediately for Oswego, where they worked nonstop to make the fort ready for an attack. During breaks in their labor, Brant expressed to the commanding officer, Major John Ross, that he feared that the British would not win and that the Indians would be left with nothing. Ross, who knew that Brant was probably right, could offer no comfort.

When the repairs were completed, Brant and his men headed south to make the customary raids on rebel settlements. This time, however, he found little to attack. The rebels were either holed up in their forts or had fled to safer places. To make matters worse, halfway through the expedition, Brant received a message from Major Ross calling him back to Oswego. It explained that a sort of cease-fire had been declared between the British and rebels.

Brant returned to Oswego bitterly disappointed. However, he was soon too busy acting as an emissary of his people to worry about the status of the war. In mid-July, Sir John Johnson, the son of Sir William, had been named the new superintendent for Indian affairs in Canada, and Brant was elected to meet with him at Montreal to discuss issues concerning the Iroquois.

After completing his diplomatic mission, Brant heard of an impending rebel attack on the Indians of Sandusky. As he had done many times before, Brant charged off, ready to join in the battle. At Sandusky, though, he discovered that the rumors of a confrontation there had been baseless. The rebels suddenly seemed uninterested in battles on the frontier. Unbeknownst to Brant, they were preoccupied with waiting for news from Europe, about peace negotiations there between the British and the Americans.

General Haldimand had an idea of what was taking place in Europe but chose to keep it to himself. It was not the prospect of peace that worried the general; it was the effect of peace on the Indians. He remembered well how peace treaties that had stripped Indians of their homeland had led to Pontiac's rebellion. Knowing the Iroquois' willingness and talent for battle, Haldimand feared what might occur if the negotiators once again ignored the concerns of their Indian allies.

5

LESSONS IN DIPLOMACY

Sir, the disposition of the Indians, and the indispensable necessity of preserving their affections may not be sufficiently understood at Home, I think it my duty to assure you that an unremitting attention to a very nice management of that People is inseparable from the safety of this Province.

These words were written by General Haldimand in a letter to the British secretary of state in London in October 1782. He hoped that they would convince the official to discuss Indian interests with the commissioners in Paris who were negotiating the treaty that would end the American Revolution. The general recognized that the Indians, deprived of their lands and driven from their country, could quite reasonably hold Britain responsible for their ills and might possibly turn violent if they were not compensated for their losses.

Unfortunately, the commissioners never saw the general's letter, and the peace treaty did not even mention the Indians. It established that the dividing line between Canada (which was still under British control) and the newly formed United States would stretch across the middle of the Great Lakes, far to the north of the boundary determined by the 1768 Treaty of Fort Stanwix.

This portrait of Brant, by John Francis Rigard, was painted in 1786 during the Mohawk leader's second visit to London. Brant was introduced to Rigard by British Indian department official General Frederick Haldimand. Haldimand later purchased the portrait and sent it as a gift to Brant for his home at Grand River.

Thus, a great deal of the old Indian country was now officially considered part of the United States by both the British and the Americans.

Haldimand tried to keep the details of the treaty from the Indians. Yet within weeks, rumors were circulating that the defeated British had betrayed their Indian allies by ceding their homelands to the rebels. Some Indians refused to believe this could be true. After all, the Indians were allies of the king, not his subjects. They reasoned that he could not possibly think he had the power to grant rights to their property to the Americans.

Brant, however, knew better. He immediately charged that "England had sold the Indians to Congress" and quickly arranged a meeting in Quebec with Sir John Johnson and General Haldimand. There, Brant delivered a powerful speech in which he demanded to know "whether those Lands which the great being above has pointed out for our Ancestors & their Descendents . . . where the Bones of our Forefathers are Laid is secured to [the Americans]."

Haldimand was caught in an awkward position. Because the Indians were not mentioned in the treaty, he could not say with any certainty what their fate would be. In a desperate attempt to appease Brant, Haldimand proposed that the Mohawks relocate to Canada and then authorized a pension of £100 a year for Brant's sister, Molly. Apparently, the idea of resettling in Canada appealed to Brant. His people were now dispossessed, so the prospect of new land, although not the land of their forefathers, was desirable. Brant's only other real option was to accept the Senecas' recent offer to share their homeland. This territory, however, was located south of the Canadian border, so it would be vulnerable to American invasions.

Haldimand sent Brant and Major Samuel Holland, the surveyor general of Canada, on an expedition along the north shore of Lake Ontario to find a suitable place for the Mohawks to live. Before they could, some Mohawk leaders decided to request a tract of land near the Bay of Quinte—a long, winding waterway that began at the northeast corner of Lake Ontario. When the Senecas heard of this choice, they became angry. Not only had the Mohawks snubbed them by refusing their generous offer to share land; they had now decided to move to a distant location, thereby threatening the very unity of the Iroquois. The Seneca leaders felt that the Iroquois' survival depended on the tribes staying close together.

Unlike the other Mohawk leaders, Brant agreed. He set about finding a suitable tract of land closer to the Senecas. He proposed to Sir John Johnson that the Mohawks settle along the Grand River, a region about 40 miles west of the Seneca settlement at Buffalo Creek. The Bay of Quinte and the Grand River selections were both approved by the British government, and both were settled by Mohawks.

In the spring of 1783, Brant submitted to Haldimand a request of compensation for losses suffered by the Mohawks in the American Revolution. In Brant's estimation, the war had cost his people more than £16,000. Haldimand was eager to help. He realized that it was important for England to reassure the Indians that they could be counted on for monetary, if not military, support. Haldimand knew as well that a unified and prosperous Iroquois settlement along lower Lake Ontario would serve as a buffer zone between Canada and the United States. He gave the Mohawks £1,500 for a start and promised to send off a request to London for the remaining amount. He also offered them tools and seeds and the services of a schoolmaster and a clergyman and arranged to have a church built at Grand River.

Brant appreciated Haldimand's generosity, but he pressed still further. The Indians needed to be assured of

This sketch of the school at Grand River appeared as the frontispiece of A Primer for the Use of the Mohawk Children, *which was prepared by Brant's friend Daniel Claus. The students and the teacher are dressed in European clothing. However, both the girls and the boys wear traditional Mohawk earrings and hairstyles.*

British protection should American settlers make claims against Indian land, Brant insisted. Haldimand again evaded the issue and denied that the king had given up the Indians' land to the Americans. The only definite information that Brant could get on the matter came from Haldimand's secretary, Major Robert Mathews. Mathews confided to Brant that the only way that the British would lend military aid to the Indians was if the Americans attacked them on the Canadian side of the border.

The prospect of facing the Americans without the British on their side certainly frightened Brant. It became clear to him that the Iroquois and their Indian neighbors needed to forget their age-old disputes and present their common enemy with a united front. Brant began to urge the leaders of some 35 Indian nations to come together under Iroquois leadership.

On September 8, 1783, his dream of an Indian confederacy became a reality. Delegates from Indian nations came from near and far to meet at Sandusky for this momentous occasion. There were Wyandots, Delawares, Hurons, Shawnees, Mingoes, Chippewas, and Ottawas from the north, Miamis from the west, the Iroquois from the east, and Creeks and Cherokees from the south.

During the council, Brant delivered a rousing speech in which he declared, "[Let] there be Peace or War, it shall never disunite us, for our interests are alike." Still, some delegates were suspicious of Brant's vision. They were worried that the Iroquois might abuse their new-found power.

No one, however, was more concerned than the Americans—they dreaded the thought of continued war with the Indians. In an attempt to avoid possible confrontations, General Philip Schuyler sent a message of peace to the Iroquois. Brant replied with an equal show of goodwill, assuring Schuyler that it was the wish of the Indian confederacy to live in peace, just as long as the Americans left Indian lands alone. Schuyler, perhaps angered by the tone of Brant's letter, sent back a message that reminded Brant and the other Iroquois leaders that they were in no position to make demands.

As the Indian sachems waited to be called to a peace council by the U.S. Congress, they received a similar request from Governor George Clinton of New York. This greatly confused the Indians. They did not know who was in charge—the Congress or the heads of the individual states. Unfortunately, neither did the Americans.

The Iroquois leaders decided to meet with both. Brant sensed that a divided American government could be used to the Indians' advantage. After all, the Indians had benefited in the past when caught in the middle of opposing governments.

General Haldimand and Sir John Johnson agreed that Brant and the Iroquois should make peace with the Americans. However, they warned the Indians not to form any alliances with either the Americans or the French. It was clear to Brant that not everyone could be pleased. He then quickly decided that if he had to act in one single group's interest, it had better be the Indians'. Although Brant was still an officer of the British Indian department and drawing a commission from it, he was beginning to see that the Indians as a group would not necessarily profit from continued allegiance to the British.

On June 6, 1784, Indian delegates and New York commissioners met at German Flats to discuss plans for the peace conference. The Indians were represented by members of the Iroquois tribes, led by Brant, and a few Delawares. Acting on instructions given to him by Haldimand, Brant proposed that the conference site be moved to the more centrally located Fort Stanwix so that representatives of all the Indian nations could be present. Brant also stated that the Indians would negotiate only with representatives of the federal government.

Governor Clinton was extremely offended when he heard the news. He considered the Indians to be a defeated people and felt that they should be more submissive in the peace negotiations. Clinton insisted that the peace council take place with only representatives of New York negotiating with the Indians. The governor also instructed one of his commissioners to discover any jealousies existing between Brant and other Indian leaders and to "promote [them] as much as you prudently can." Clinton had rightly sensed that the other nations were wary of the Iroquois and that they resented Joseph

Brant, the Mohawk of low birth who acted like a sachem, most of all.

The Indian leaders agreed to Clinton's terms, and the peace negotiations at Fort Stanwix got under way in early September 1784. But Brant soon saw that the New York commissioners were more concerned with obtaining Indian land than lasting peace. They demanded land near Oswego and Niagara and sought to draw boundaries around Indian-occupied land within the state. The commissioners argued that because the Indians had been responsible for many injustices against the Americans during the war, they should be forced to give up land as reparation.

As usual, Brant spoke out on the Indians' behalf. He declared that the Indians would not enter into any agreement until a formal peace had been reached with the U.S. Congress. Concerning the land cessions, Brant explained that he had to consult with other Indian leaders before any deals could be made. He also did his best to establish a friendship with Governor Clinton. Somewhat naively, Brant still hoped that he could regain the Mohawk land at Canajoharie. Apparently, he did not know that his childhood home had already been overrun by white settlers. The conference ended with little determined.

During the negotiations, Brant's wife, Catharine, had given birth to a son at Fort Niagara. But Brant could not make the trip to see their firstborn right away. He had urgent business to conduct with Haldimand in Quebec before the general returned to England. Brant wanted written documentation of the land grant at Grand River. The Mohawk leader also hoped to convince Haldimand to allow him to go to England as well. He wanted to talk with the king about the possibility of war with the Americans and about obtaining the £14,500 still due the

Mohawks. Brant succeeded in getting Haldimand to sign over the Grand River land, but his plans to go with the general had to be postponed. Disaster had struck at Fort Stanwix.

The Americans at the fort had taken several hostages, proclaiming that they would be held until all American prisoners captured during the war were released. The hostages included a Mohawk leader and personal friend of Brant's, Aaron Hill, and five other chiefs. Even though the captive leaders argued that they had no power to do so, American treaty commissioners began to pressure the captives to sign over territory in western Pennsylvania and eastern Ohio. In the end, the hostages were forced to sell all of the land that the Iroquois claimed in Pennsylvania. The tract held the Indians' best hunting grounds, and they were paid only $5,000 for it.

The purchase was a strategic victory for the Americans. Not only had they acquired valuable land; they had severely disrupted the unity of the Indian confederacy. A Seneca chief, Abeel Cornplanter, had played a major part in the land cession, so internal strife threatened to divide the Iroquois as well. In fact, tensions grew so great that Cornplanter feared for his life and tried to get the Americans to void the land cession. Instead, however, more land cessions followed. The Indian confederacy seemed incapable of acting as a unified whole, and resentments increased among its members. A strong leader was needed to bring the situation under control, and it was becoming increasingly clear that Joseph Brant was the best man for the job.

However, during 1784, Brant had more than his share of problems serving simply as leader of the Mohawks. He had been successful in gaining legal title to the Grand River territory, but the Mohawks' subsequent relocation was troublesome. Their Indian neighbors there, the

Seneca chief Abeel Cornplanter undercut Brant's authority in 1784 by ceding Iroquois hunting grounds in Pennsylvania to the United States without first obtaining the permission of Brant and the other Iroquois leaders. For many years after, Brant and Cornplanter were bitter political rivals.

Missisaugas, were not terribly welcoming to the Mohawks, owing to old rivalries between the two peoples. The Mohawks also found that a few white Tories had already settled on Grand River land. Brant had encouraged them because he felt that the Indians would benefit from their agricultural knowledge. The Tories had agreed readily—the land was fertile, game was plentiful, and the river provided easy transportation to Lake Erie. Despite their troubles, such surroundings made the loss of the Mohawks' ancient homeland slightly easier to bear.

Once the settlement at Grand River was off to a good start, Brant left for Quebec. Sir John Johnson was due to return from England, and Brant was eager to learn whether the requests to the king that he had conveyed to Haldimand had been answered. He was waiting on the pier when Sir John's ship came, but found that Johnson had not brought good news. Indeed, Johnson evaded Brant's questions, telling him only that he had been awarded a half pension for his services to the British Indian department. Brant was far from satisfied with this answer. Despite Johnson's attempts to dissuade him, Brant made up his mind to go to England himself.

He set sail aboard the *Madona* on November 6, 1785. After a monthlong journey, Brant disembarked at Salisbury and set off for London by coach. Unlike during his first trip to England, Brant now had a reputation to precede him. The British press heralded the coming of Joseph Brant, "King of the Mohawks," and rumored that Brant had brought the news that war would soon break out between the Indians and the Americans.

Brant's first appointment was with British secretary of state Lord Sydney and a few British Indian department officials, including Guy Johnson and Daniel Claus, with whom Brant was lodging. The meetings began smoothly,

despite Brant's insistence on speaking through a trans-
lator. Sydney confirmed that the payment to the
Mohawks for their wartime losses was on its way. Brant
then spoke of recent American encroachments on Indian
territory and again reminded Sydney of the Indians' role
in the war. He also brought up the matter of his captain's
commission, which entitled him to a full annual pension,
not the half he had been offered. Lastly, Brant put to
Sydney the question that he had traveled so far to ask:
"We desire to know whether we are to be considered as
his majesty's faithful Allies, and have that Support and
Countenance, Such old true friends expect?" Sydney gave
him the usual British official's response—he could give
no immediate answer.

By the spring of 1786, Brant had begun to tire of
waiting. The irate Brant later wrote in his diary:

*The Grand River settlement
along the Mohawk River as it
appeared in 1800. Although
Brant and the other Mohawk
residents of Grand River
missed their ancestral territory,
fertile land and abundant
resources helped them quickly
thrive in their new home.*

> The more I know of this country, the more I see that it is
> the height of folly to trust to the generosity of the [British]
> nation. Services are forgotten the moment there is no
> longer need of us.

He again brought his complaints to Haldimand, who suggested he speak with his old rival Sir Guy Carleton, the new governor of Canada. Carleton assisted Brant in his inquiries about his pension, only to find that no decision had been made. Brant then angrily declined the half-pension, saying that if there were doubts about whether he deserved the full amount, he would not accept anything.

Brant also reminded the governor of his year-old request for the Mohawks' war reparations. Carleton, who understood the value of the Indian alliance to the security of Canada, succeeded in getting Brant nearly £15,000 for his people and promised that the Mohawks would receive additional presents.

Brant had less success with his request for British military support. He left England without a firm statement from Sydney on the matter. It was not that the British themselves were unsure. They knew that they no longer had the power to aid the Indians, and they could no longer afford to antagonize the Americans. The only subject for debate was how best to break the news to the Indians and salvage the alliance for the sake of Canada.

Sydney and his fellow deliberators came to a conclusion sometime shortly before Brant set sail. In carefully chosen words, Sydney told Brant that the king "shall at all times be ready to attend to [the Indians] future welfare." Brant had dealt with the British long enough to be able to grasp Sydney's real message—the Indians should resolve their disputes peaceably with the Americans. If it came to war, they could expect no help from the British. The outnumbered and poorly equipped Indians were on their own.

Brant reached Niagara in early July 1786 and found that war between the Indians and the Americans was imminent. The Shawnees had been driven from their land in Ohio by combined forces under General Richard Butler, head of the American Indian department, and frontiersman George Rogers Clark. As a result, the western boundary of the United States had been extended to the border of present-day Indiana.

In response, parties of Mingoes and Cherokees attacked settlements in Ohio and Kentucky. Bands of warriors set out almost daily from Detroit, bringing back scalps and prisoners. Many of these Indians thought that British military help would soon be on the way. As a result, they did not fear American reprisals. But they soon would. The newly formed American militia, led by Clark and Colonel Benjamin Logan, made sure that each Indian raid was avenged.

While these raids were taking place, Brant was busy organizing a council of all the leaders of the Indian confederacy. Realizing that the Indians could not win a war without British support, he urged the Indians who attended to sue for peace. Once again, Brant delivered a powerful speech, encouraging the Indians to unite and rallying them to action:

> We were the lords of the soil, the great Spirit placed us there! and what is the reason, why are we not still in posses-
> sion of our forefathers birth rights?

The council drew up a message and sent it off to the Congress on December 18, 1786. It stated firmly that the Indians were not conquered peoples and should not have to give up their lands. They proposed that a peace-treaty council be held in the coming spring and declared invalid any treaties that had already been signed by individual Indian leaders.

Seven months passed before the U.S. Congress turned its attention to the Indians' message. In that time, new settlements had sprung up in Ohio, and many more Indian attacks had taken place. Indeed, the war that Brant had hoped to avert was now virtually taking place on the Ohio frontier. Furthermore, Congress passed the Northwest Ordinance, which set up a government for the land in Ohio and began dividing up western lands into individual states.

Meanwhile, British officials in Canada were doing their best to promote Indian unity, supplying them with food, supplies, and ammunition. Although the British were not willing to send their own troops, they hoped the Indians could help them retain their western forts and keep the prosperous fur trade flowing. Yet the official British position was that the Indians should avoid war.

If anyone was willing to make a real attempt to stop the fighting, it was Joseph Brant. He was able to convince the western Indians during a council at Fort Huron to restrain their young warriors and to honor the dictates of the confederacy. Brant also tried to remove a major source of anger among the Americans—Indian control of British forts on American territory. Brant urged the British government to turn the forts over to the U.S. government, but his words fell on deaf ears. The British explained to Brant that the fur trade depended on control of the forts and that they could not be given up. Brant quickly realized that he would have to act without British approval. He now knew what he had previously only suspected—his loyalty to the king had to be sacrificed to the interests of his people.

The issue of having to defend the British forts never arose, however, because the U.S. Congress found a means of resolving the problem. Congress no more wanted a war than did the Indians. So in late October 1787 it began appropriating money for the purchase of Indian territory. Unfortunately, it did not occur to the American leaders that the Indians might not want to sell their land.

Fort Harmar, the site of a 1789 treaty council that spelled the end of any hope for an enduring peace between Indians and whites on the western frontier. At the fort, Cornplanter and several other Indian leaders signed away large tracts of land in the West. Despite the treaty, the Indian inhabitants of the ceded areas had no intention of leaving the region without a fight.

6

A DISH WITH ONE SPOON

At the close of 1787, Indian scouts in Ohio began to report sightings of boatloads of American settlers. On the heels of these reports, Americans began to construct a new fort at the mouth of the Muskingum River. Fort Harmar, as it was called, was established to help protect the newcomers from Indian raids.

The fort's commander, General Josiah Harmar, was warned also to be on his guard when dealing with Joseph Brant and the Indian confederacy. Arthur St. Clair, the new governor of the Ohio territory, wrote Harmar that "every exertion must be made to defeat all confederations and combinations among the tribes."

The Indians in Ohio were shocked by the tremendous wave of settlers. Some responded by calling for a formal peace with the Americans; others advocated reacting to the intrusion with violence. All agreed, however, that a council must take place as soon as possible. Brant promptly arranged for a conference to be held at the rapids of the Maumee River and invited Governor St. Clair to attend.

In preparation for the meeting, Brant drew up his own solution to settling the dispute over the Ohio territory. Sensing that compromise would be the best approach, he decided that the confederacy should offer the Americans all of the land east of the Muskingum River. The Ohio Indians would lose a great deal of land by this plan, but they would be able to retain enough territory west of the river to survive.

Unfortunately for Brant, the chances for compromise were severely damaged before the council even convened. In July 1787, a group of St. Clair's soldiers, who had been sent down to watch over the council site, were attacked by Indian warriors. St. Clair was enraged. He ordered that the council be moved to Fort Harmar and, unknown to the Indians, began planning for war against the Indian confederacy.

Before traveling to Fort Harmar, the Indian council representatives conferred at the Maumee rapids. This meeting quickly turned sour, with many of the western Indians objecting to the presence of the Iroquois. Instead of solidifying their position, the representatives left the rapids sharply divided over what they should demand from St. Clair as the terms for peace. Some of the Indians were so frustrated that they saw no point in even bothering to continue on to Fort Harmar.

Believing that these representatives might be afraid to travel to the council site, Brant then wrote to St. Clair and asked that the council be held at the falls of the Muskingum instead of the American fort. St. Clair flatly refused the request. Possibly angered by the governor's obstinacy, Brant called the council off altogether and merely sent St. Clair a copy of the speech he had been intending to make that outlined his plan for the Muskingum boundary. Again, St. Clair rejected Brant's proposal.

Despite the cancellation of the council and against the wishes of most of the Indian nations, Seneca chief Abeel Cornplanter, a rival of Brant's, led a group of Indians to meet with St. Clair at Fort Harmar in January 1789.

There, Cornplanter and other Indian leaders present blamed Brant for the current hostilities between Indians and Americans. They also accused him of planning an attack on Fort Pitt and said that he did not represent the true interests of the confederacy.

St. Clair saw that, unlike Brant, the leaders of this delegation were fairly compliant. He took advantage of the situation by immediately drawing up two peace treaties whose terms were very favorable to the United States. In the documents, the land cessions to the Americans made in previous treaties were confirmed. In return, the Indians were paid $9,000. When Cornplanter and the others returned to their people, they reported only that they had signed a peace treaty. They said nothing of the land cessions, explaining that the payments were mere presents. Very possibly, these leaders did not understand the terms of the treaties and left Fort Harmar thinking that they had in fact signed over no land.

Later in the year, a delegation of western Indians visited Brant at Grand River to seek his advice. They apologized for acting independently of the Indian confederacy at Fort Harmar. Brant told them that he could only speak for the Iroquois (excluding the Senecas) and that they should always feel free to act without asking his opinion. If the Americans encroach upon your land, said Brant, then you must act swifty in any manner that you see fit. These statements suggest that, disappointed by his dealings with St. Clair, Brant now had thoughts of relinquishing his role as principal representative of the confederacy and all the burdens that it entailed.

That winter, Brant had enough trouble with a fresh dispute that had erupted between the Iroquois and the state of New York. The Onondagas, Cayugas, and Oneidas were contesting the sale of a tract of land to New York by Indians who had not consulted with the Iroquois leadership first. They were particularly angered because, in violation of Iroquois custom, the sellers kept the money they obtained instead of turning it over to the Iroquois leadership so it could be used by the nation as a whole.

Brant wrote an angry letter to New York governor Clinton demanding that the surveying of the disputed lands be halted immediately. Clinton answered that the treaties were fair and refused to renegotiate. Brant wrote back accusing the governor of making the purchases behind the backs of the Iroquois leaders, reminding Clinton that the Indians held their land in common and sales made by unauthorized Indians were invalid. He also accused Clinton of trying to turn the Indians against each other. Brant was determined that the debacle at Fort Harmar not be repeated.

In the summer of 1790, Brant finally reached an agreement with Clinton whereby the land sales stood but the Indians received proper compensation for the ceded territory. Clinton's dealings with the Mohawk leader in this affair produced a strong impression on the governor, prompting him to write to President Washington that Brant was "a man of considerable information, influence and enterprize, and in my humble opinion, his Friendship is worthy of cultivation." The once-feared Brant was now recognized by the Americans as a diplomat through whom peaceable Indian relations could be achieved.

Meanwhile, on the western frontier, Indians unhappy with the Fort Harmar treaties were resorting to violence. One instance began when St. Clair sent a French agent to the villages of the Miami Indians to negotiate the sale of some land. The agent was burned alive by the Miamis, who accused St. Clair of trying to cheat them, given that the governor knew all land deals had to be made with the Indian confederacy.

Hearing of this atrocity, St. Clair and Harmar set out to bring the Miami villages under American control. With

Arthur St. Clair, the governor of Ohio territory, did little to endear himself to Brant. All the while promising peace, St. Clair continually plotted to destroy the Indian confederacy Brant had created.

more than 1,600 soldiers, they left Fort Washington (present-day Cincinnati) in September 1790 with the hope of catching the Miamis and their allies, the Shawnees, by surprise. Near what is now Fort Wayne, Indiana, St. Clair's army of 1,300 encountered the Indians' forces. They drove the warriors back but suffered many casualties. Although the Indians were greatly outnumbered and had only tomahawks, spears, and bows and arrows as weapons, they had the advantage of knowing the thickly wooded terrain. The Indians also were experienced fighters, whereas many of the Americans ran at the first sign of danger. Ultimately, the American army retreated.

St. Clair returned home, loudly declaring that the expedition had been a success and downplaying the magnitude of his defeat at Fort Wayne. Later, when the true number of American losses became known, the battle was called "Harmar's defeat." Back in Ohio, however, the Miamis and Shawnees always knew who had won at Fort Wayne. The victory gave them renewed confidence in their ability to fight off American expansionism.

But when Brant learned of the battle out west, he was anything but optimistic. One small victory, he realized, could cost the Indians many more defeats in the future. Brant knew that the Americans would return to fight the Miamis and Shawnees again, and with a much larger army. He wrote to his new friend, Governor Clinton, that the battle would never have taken place if St. Clair had not taken so much of their land. But more important than telling Clinton, "I told you so," Brant now had to decide whether the Iroquois should join their brothers in the west in a war. He knew that the Indians could not possibly win such a conflict. Yet, if the Iroquois did not join them, the Indian confederacy could be divided permanently.

A change in American Indian policy suddenly made it appear that Brant might not have to make this difficult decision, after all. Possibly fearing that British officials would try to intervene in their disagreements with the Indians, the Americans decided to try to compromise in cases of territorial dispute. To pacify the Indians, they began offering money for land instead of annexing it, dealing with authorized Indians leaders instead of swindling those unauthorized to sell land, and even passing fair trade laws.

The new policies did not sway the western Indians toward peace, however. They meant to retain their land whether the Americans offered them money for it or not. Thus, when a British diplomat, Colonel Andrew Gordon, traveled to Ohio and offered to negotiate with the United States on their behalf, they refused his help. The only British aid they wanted was military aid.

Brant accompanied Gordon on this diplomatic mission and stayed on in Ohio after the colonel departed. Fearing that the American army might strike at any moment, the western Indians asked him to go to Quebec to find out how much support they could expect from the British officials there. Although he was opposed to the war, Brant agreed. He knew that he could not ignore the wishes of the Shawnees and Miamis without calling into question his own loyalty to the Indian confederacy.

Brant arrived in Quebec near the end of July 1791 and immediately met with Guy Carleton, who, now known as Lord Dorchester, was serving as the governor of Lower Canada. Using the familiar argument that the Indians had fought nobly on the side of the British in the American Revolution, Brant tried to secure military aid. In addition, he asked that forts be built at the Maumee rapids and at Detroit for Indian protection. Brant also seized this opportunity to repropose the Muskingum boundary, stating that if the American expansion did not stop there, it would not stop until all Indian land was taken away. Dorchester told Brant that he was going to sail to England in a week and that he would advise the king of these demands.

Even before Dorchester could cross the Atlantic, fighting broke out all over Virginia, Kentucky, and Pennsylvania. White settlers were attacked in their fields, in their farmhouses, and in the woods. The Americans quickly organized counterattacks, but at the same time they also sent out diplomats to try to avoid further bloodshed.

A watercolor of Brant, painted in about 1794. In the portrait, Brant is wearing a medal that was probably presented to him by King George III. By the early 1790s, however, Brant's loyalty to the British was wavering as he detected their unwillingness to lend his Indian confederacy any military support.

Again, money was offered to the Indians in an effort to appease them. But the real issue was land, and neither side would budge.

Meanwhile, St. Clair renewed his attempts at thwarting the unity of the Indian confederacy and began planning a major campaign against the western Indians. Knowing that St. Clair was on the way, the Indians eagerly awaited Brant's return and his report on his meeting with Dorchester. Much to their irritation, Brant never arrived. Instead, messengers from him passed along word that the western Indians should expect no military aid from the British.

Undaunted, the Miamis joined up with another group of Indians, made up mostly of Shawnees and a few Iroquois, to form a war party of about 1,000 men. Early in the morning on November 4, 1791, this combined Indian force attacked St. Clair's army near the present day Indiana-Ohio border. The element of surprise worked to the advantage of the slightly outnumbered Indians. After a brief and deadly skirmish during which half of St. Clair's men were killed, the Americans retreated.

Among those wounded was the much-despised Richard Butler, the superintendent of Indian affairs for the United States. Butler's role in what the Indians saw as shady land dealings and illegal treaties did not serve him well as their prisoner. When Brant returned home to Grand River, Butler's scalp was awaiting him. With it was a message denouncing Brant as a traitor.

Whatever respect the western Indians may have had for Joseph Brant appeared now to be lost. Not only had he failed to obtain British military support; he had not even bothered to deliver the news in person, nor did he join his brothers on the battlefield. The western Indians felt that Brant was more devoted to the English than he was to the Indian confederacy.

As if these accusations were not devastating enough for Brant, he became seriously ill less than a month after returning to Grand River. His prognosis was so bad that many feared for his life. However, Brant was placed under the care of an excellent physician at Fort Niagara and soon began to recover his strength.

During his recuperation, Brant received a letter from Secretary of War Henry Knox stating that the United States wanted to end the war and that it desired no more Indian land. By January 1792, the ailing leader was well enough to set off for Philadelphia, then the nation's capital, to discuss this latest turn of events with officials there.

Although heartened by the Americans' new apparent willingness to compromise, Brant traveled with some trepidation. The trip down to Philadelphia was dangerous. In many of the settlements he passed through, he was regarded as something of a monster for his ferocity during the American Revolution. The possibility that some settlers might seek revenge against Brant was very real. The journey also marked the first time Brant had been to Canajoharie since it had been settled by whites. The village had changed so drastically, with woodland cleared for pastures and farmhouses in place of Indian longhouses, that he hardly recognized his boyhood home.

Finally reaching Philadelphia on June 20, Brant was greeted enthusiastically by the federal officials he met. They offered him many presents and large sums of money if he would work to prevent further violence by the western Indians. Secretary Knox was especially congenial. Knox wanted to prove the good intentions of the government toward the Indians, largely because the American populace was now demanding that peace be made.

In his meetings with Knox, Brant again recommended establishing the Muskingum line as the official boundary between the United States and Canada. Knox, knowing that land west of the Muskingum had already been settled, argued instead for the boundary set by the Fort Harmar treaty. The outcome of their discussions was six peace proposals, which Brant was to present to the western Indians as the basis of a lasting treaty. Although the list was supposedly coauthored by Brant and Knox, it was clearly more the work of the secretary.

According to the proposals, the United States would keep the land ceded at Fort Harmar. However, the Indians would be paid for all land west of the Muskingum River and for all other territory now belonging to the United States for which they had not been properly compensated in the past. Also, agricultural experts would be sent to teach the Indians to raise crops and cattle.

Before taking Knox's proposals to the confederacy, Brant showed them to George Hammond, a British minister to the United States who was then stationed in Philadelphia. Brant confided to Hammond that the warring Indians were unlikely to agree to them, although the promise of money and presents might lure others into approving the proposals against their better judgment, thereby causing a rift in the confederacy.

During a stop in New York on his way back to Grand River, an event occurred that justified Brant's fears about traveling so deeply into U.S. territory. A man named Dygert, who had lost several members of his family in the Brant-led raid on German Flats during the American Revolution, made an attempt on his life. A friend of Brant's named Colonel Marinus Willett, who noticed Dygert following Brant in a suspicious manner, prevented the assassination. Brant was reportedly very disturbed by the whole affair and, with good reason, left New York in a hurry.

Brant returned to Niagara on July 24, prepared to hear the reproaches of the Iroquois leaders for undertaking a

Red Jacket, a Seneca leader well known for his eloquence, convinced the western Indians to consider peace proposals drawn up by Brant and Secretary of War Henry Knox. Unfortunately, the Indians' mistrust of Americans was already so deep that they were ultimately unable to take any peace overtures from the United States seriously.

diplomatic mission without first consulting them. Although he was sharply criticized, his diplomacy was also praised by those who had heard of his stern negotiations with Knox. Yet he still had to face the western Indians, who he feared might denounce him despite his success in Philadelphia. Thus, as a precaution, Brant sent his son Isaac to Ohio with the peace proposals instead of going himself.

In the meantime, Knox had sent his own men west to find out if the Indians were ready for peace. Three of these emissaries were killed by suspicious Indian scouts, but two others managed to reach the Wabash Indian leaders and persuade them to meet and discuss Knox's proposals. In early September 1792, representatives of the Shawnees, Cherokees, Miamis, and Delawares joined the Wabash Indians along the Auglaize River near present-day Defiance, Ohio. There, they settled in, waiting for Brant to come with news of his Philadelphia negotiations.

Isaac arrived at the Auglaize a few days later, but instead of relating the peace proposals, he said that he and his party had come to join the Indians in war. Isaac also maintained that his father advised them to ignore Knox's plan. (It is not known whether Isaac acted on his own or whether he was actually following secret instructions from his father. If Brant truly desired peace, the communication made by Isaac could not have come from him.)

Only through a series of speeches made by the Seneca chief Red Jacket were the peace proposals put back on the agenda. Still, Red Jacket's eloquence was not enough to counter the attending Indians' mistrust of the Americans. The previous summer they had intercepted orders from General St. Clair that called for the expulsion of all violent tribes from Ohio. Because the orders contradicted everything contained in the proposals, the Indians found it difficult to believe in Knox's plan for peace. The council ended with the Indians drawing up their own proposals, in which they demanded that all American forts in Ohio be abandoned and that their land be returned. For once, all members of the confederation were in agreement.

Brant himself arrived at the Auglaize shortly after the council had broken up. He told the remaining Indians what had happened in Philadelphia, but his story changed nothing. The next day, Shawnee and Wyandot warriors began to prepare for war. Brant worked to delay the fighting, again arguing for compromise and the Muskingum boundary but again receiving little response. On November 8, he returned to Grand River, expecting war to break out any moment.

Once back at home, Brant received a visitor—John Simcoe, the new lieutenant governor of Upper Canada (today the Province of Ontario). Simcoe explained that he wanted to establish a lasting boundary between the United States and Canada that would safely put the Indians between the two nations. Somewhat ignorant of Brant's failed attempts to establish the Muskingum River as such a border, Simcoe proposed the Ohio River as the best geographic boundary. Through this scheme, the western Indians would be able to retain even more land than they would with Brant's.

At the well-attended council of the Indian confederacy at the Maumee rapids in March 1793, the western Indians enthusiastically endorsed Simcoe's plan. Undaunted, Brant spoke out against it. He felt that asking the Americans to concede all land east of the Muskingum River was too great a demand. Brant also wanted to stipulate in any peace agreement that no land could be sold without the consent of the confederacy in the future. To support this demand, Brant cited an old adage that their land was a "dish with one spoon," meaning that it was a possession that they all shared. Hoping to reestablish his credibility with the western Indians, Brant closed his speech stating that the Indian confederacy was "the first wish of [my] heart."

But some Indians remained suspicious of Brant's allegiances. The Shawnees, for instance, were spreading rumors that Brant was receiving bribes from the

Americans. Whether he believed these accusations or not, Alexander McKee encouraged these rumors in order to erode Brant's influence. Simcoe knew better than to suspect Brant of conspiring with the Americans, but he too was afraid that Brant might thwart the acceptance of his own terms for peace.

On July 21, at Niagara, a delegation from the Indian confederacy met with a group of Americans who were fully empowered to set the new boundary. One faction among the delegates produced a document that would establish the Ohio River as the boundary, but the Iroquois representatives, including Brant, refused to sign it. Hos-

An engraving of General Anthony Wayne's victory against the western Indians in the Battle of Fallen Timbers. With this defeat, the Indians of Ohio lost any chance of retaining their homelands.

tility then broke out among the Indian delegates, and all left the conference deeply disgruntled. Once again, the inability of the various Indian tribes to agree with one another ruined a good chance for peace.

Later that year, another delegation, headed by the Delaware chief Buckongehala, met at Maumee with a group of American commissioners, to whom they presented their demand for the Ohio River boundary. The commissioners told Buckongehala that his proposal was unacceptable, that they could not give up land already bought and settled by whites. However, the Americans were willing to give up all the land west of the Ohio River that had not been settled, which included everything except the settlements at Marietta, Gallipolis, and Cincinnati. Buckongehala dismissed the offer, declaring that he refused to compromise.

The other Indian representatives decided to discuss the Americans' terms with their tribes. The issue came down to either accepting Brant's Muskingum boundary or holding fast and insisting on the Ohio River boundary. After long debates, the various Indian groups seemed ready to consent to Brant's plan. But suddenly the Shawnee, Delaware, and Huron chiefs changed their minds. Brant later found out from Buckongehala that Alexander McKee had persuaded these chiefs to demand the Ohio River boundary. A deeply frustrated Brant left the council the next day, wishing the western Indians luck in the upcoming war.

After Brant's departure, the remaining Indian leaders at Maumee produced an ultimatum to send to Philadelphia. Signed by 16 Indian nations, this message put matters simply: "Restore to us our country, and we shall be enemies no longer." These uncompromising demands betrayed a lack of the type of diplomacy that Brant alone among the Indians seemed to possess. Of course, these were exactly the demands that the Americans were unwilling to accept.

The Indians' obstinacy was especially unfortunate, because at the time the United States would have been happier than ever to strike a compromise in order to avert more fighting. In Europe, war had broken out between England and France. Because the Americans had thrown their support behind the French, they feared that the British would soon declare war on the United States. If the British and the Indians combined their forces and defeated the Americans, the victors could demand any boundary they wished.

Early in 1794, Britain appeared on the verge of giving military aid to the Indians. Fearing this, President Washington sent one of his officers to bribe Brant in order to prevent a council from taking place at Niagara. It is unknown whether Brant accepted the bribe or not, but the council did convene.

Washington also dispatched John Jay, the chief justice of the Supreme Court, to England to try to negotiate a new peace treaty. It was too late, however, to avert more warfare at home. In June 1794, about 2,000 Indians prepared to ambush the army of General Anthony Wayne, which was headed for the Auglaize River. While waiting, a few parties of warriors attempted small-scale attacks on Wayne's army. These warriors meant to surprise the Americans and reduce their numbers, but the Indians suffered the most casualties in these skirmishes.

At the mouth of the Auglaize, the full force of Wayne's army met the Indians at the Battle of Fallen Timbers. Unfortunately for the Indians, a large number of their warriors had gone to get supplies from Alexander McKee, leaving only 1,300 warriors to face the Americans. Seeing themselves outnumbered, many warriors fled the battlefield. (McKee later said that just 400 Indians stayed to fight.) The battle was brief, and the Indians were routed.

While the United States and England were ironing out their own peace in London, the western Indians were utterly ruined. Wayne's troops burned all of the Indian villages in the region (McKee's house was also reduced to ashes), and an American fort went up in their place—Fort Defiance. Fearing that Wayne's army was soon coming their way, the inhabitants of Indian villages west of the Auglaize River moved farther west, some into Tennessee, others across the Mississippi River into Spanish territory. In one violent turn of events, the Indians of Ohio had lost everything.

7

To Do the Indians Good

With the loss of Ohio and the decay of the Indian confederacy, Brant turned his attention to his own settlement at Grand River. Now known as Brant's Town to its residents, the community was prospering. It had a church, a school, and many thriving farms. Brant even had succeeded in getting many of the Mohawks there inoculated against smallpox. Nevertheless, the settlement did have some problems of its own—problems that were perhaps too great even for someone of Brant's power and influence to solve.

Brant's Town had survived many near catastrophes in the late 1780s. Because they were restricted to the boundaries of the settlement, the residents could do little hunting, fostering a dependence on farming and trade for food. A crop failure in 1788 thus had caused many people to abandon their farms. Altercations often broke out between the Indians and the white settlers. (In one such incident, Joseph's son Isaac murdered a white man over a trifling matter.) Brant also had been unable to find a regular missionary for the Grand River church, so services were irregular and unpredictable. However, these problems were small when compared to one that arose in 1793.

A 1794 portrait of Brant and his dog standing on the bank of the Grand River. The artist, William De Berczy, was a German immigrant who attempted to buy Grand River land from Brant but could not meet the Mohawk leader's price.

In that year, Brant asked the British government in Canada to survey the Grand River land so that the Indians would know its exact boundaries. The surveyor, Augustus Jones, discovered that Haldimand had made a mistake in his grant of the land 11 years earlier. According to the grant, the Mohawks' land did not extend to the head-waters of the Grand River, as Haldimand had led the Mohawks to believe. Brant then decided that it was time to get an official deed for the Grand River land, one that included the land omitted by Haldimand when he drew up the grant.

Brant petitioned the British Indian department to draw up the deed, but received no response. Unbeknownst to Brant, his request was unique; the British had never given a deed for land to Indians before. The Indian department was unsure what to do, so it referred the matter to Governor Simcoe in Quebec.

Before long, Brant heard rumors that Simcoe was preparing to reduce the amount of land held by the Grand River Mohawks. Horrified, Brant wrote to the governor asking for the deed. Simcoe answered that Brant need not worry. He would see that a deed was drawn up soon. But, in fact, Simcoe had no intention of doing this. He knew it was in the best interest of the Canadian government to prevent the Indians from holding their land independently. If Indians could own their land outright, they could sell it to whomever they pleased, including Americans.

Time passed, and nothing was done. Brant finally intercepted Simcoe on a trip to Niagara and showed him the documentation of Haldimand's grant for the first time. This impressed the governor, who then made a somewhat more sincere promise to follow through with the deed. But he also told Brant that a deed was not really necessary and that the British government would honor the Mohawks' claim to their land. Knowing better than to be content with this answer, Brant kept the pressure on Simcoe.

Finally, on January 14, 1793, Simcoe presented him and the Mohawks with a deed for Grand River. However, it omitted the same important tract that had been left out of Haldimand's original grant. In addition, Simcoe added a condition that forbade the Indians to sell the land to anyone except themselves and the king of England. Brant was deeply insulted. He considered the Indians the owners of their own land, which meant that they could use the land in any way that they wished and sell it to whomever they pleased. Despite Brant's complaints, Simcoe said that the Mohawks could either accept this deed or no deed at all.

For a time, the matter rested. But in 1795 the deed question arose again when the Indians were forced to sell land in order to obtain provisions after a particularly difficult winter. Acting as a broker, Brant arranged for the sale of a 12-square-mile parcel of land, for which he received a small tract. Brant's actions were bold, but not

Brant's disillusionment with the British grew when he could not persuade officials to give him a formal deed to the Grand River settlement. He voiced his frustration in this portion of a 1793 letter, in which he wrote to his friend Alexander McKee, "I never did [expect] that my attachment to the English should any time shake. I am totally dispirited."

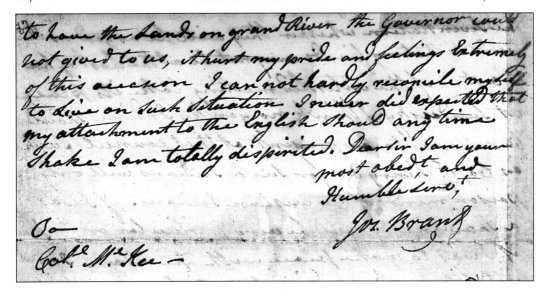

too bold, for the buyer was a British subject. Still, the sale was expressly forbidden by Simcoe's deed.

Before Simcoe could respond, Brant sold three more large blocks of land, this time at an auction to the highest bidder. Simcoe was outraged. This sort of random sale of land was what he feared most. He demanded to meet with Brant and the other Mohawk leaders at Grand River, but nothing was decided in their discussions. Simcoe would not alter the conditions of the deed, and Brant would not agree to halt the sale of Grand River land. When the meeting adjourned, Simcoe promised to refer the matter to Lord Dorchester.

Soon after, a tragedy occurred that was to change Brant's life forever. Along with many other Grand River Indians, Brant and his son Isaac traveled to Lake Ontario to greet British ships and receive their annual gifts from the traders aboard. During the trip, a fight broke out between Brant and Isaac one night. According to the report of William Johnson Chew, who was staying in the room next to Brant at an inn, Isaac was drunk and began shouting and swearing at his father. Isaac then drew a knife and took a stab at Brant, striking him on the hand. Brant then drew his own knife and hit Isaac in the head. Two days later, the young man died from his injury. Although many different stories evolved from this event, Brant probably stabbed Isaac in self-defense. In any case, Brant was shattered by the incident.

Isaac's death, however, did not lessen Brant's leadership role at Grand River. In 1796, Lord Dorchester presented him with a new deed. This document gave the Mohawks the right to sell their own land, provided that the king was allowed to make the first offer. Brant rejected the deed immediately. He explained that although he did not mind selling land to the king, he did object to the deed's naming the Iroquois as the owners of the Grand River.

It was the settlers at Grand River, and not all of the Iroquois, who rightfully owned the land, Brant argued. The deed also implied that the people of Grand River were British subjects. A frustrated Brant wrote Simcoe that, because a proper deed could not be provided, he was content to let the Haldimand grant stand as proof of ownership.

The deed dispute was temporarily over, but later in the year a new conflict emerged when the British authorities contested Brant's earlier land sales. In order to obtain payment, Brant needed to present deeds to the new owners of the tracts he sold. Unfortunately for him, both Simcoe and Dorchester had returned to London and therefore were not available to confirm the land sales and issue the documents. The new officials were hesitant to do so. They feared, just as had Simcoe, that if left unchecked Brant would sell land within Canada's borders to Americans. Brant had given them no reason to suspect this—all his land sales had been made either to Mohawks or to British subjects. Yet accusations continued to fly.

Meanwhile, word of Brant's shrewd land deals spread throughout the Iroquois nations. As a result, the 35 Iroquois chiefs voted to grant Brant power of attorney over all Iroquois land sales. This gave Brant the legal right to sell land to the British on behalf of the Iroquois in exchange for monies that would provide the Indians with an annuity—a guaranteed yearly income. This power made Brant a virtual sachem, something that an Indian of low birth could never before have hoped to achieve.

Despite this honor, Brant was still having trouble obtaining both official deeds and money for the land sales he had made. Simcoe's replacement, Peter Russell, told Brant that he needed to get the approval of the Duke of Portland before he could release the deeds. "This is not

what we deserve," Brant said, telling Russell that he would go to England himself and speak with Simcoe and Dorchester if he had to. The empty threat (Brant did not have the resources to make a trip to England) did not work. So Brant did the next best thing, and he went to Philadelphia in early 1797 to see Robert Liston, the British minister to the United States.

Brant heaped his complaints on an unprepared Liston. He then issued a new threat, one that was taken very seriously. Brant boldly swore that he would lend his services to the French should the British continue to treat him as they had. He also accused Russell of blocking his land sales in order to gain land for himself. Perhaps eager to get back to Grand River, Brant cut his visit short, even canceling a meeting with President Washington to do so.

Brant had, in fact, approached the right man with his problems. Fearing the growing influence of the French in Canada, Liston fired off letters about his meetings with

The small settlement of York, the capital of Lower Canada, was the site of one of Brant's greatest and most satisfying victories as a negotiator. In 1797 he convinced the council at York to officially approve the land sales he had made on behalf of the Mohawks, thus establishing the tribe's right to sell their own land to whomever they pleased.

the Mohawk leader to officials in Canada and England. Evidently, Liston's letters raised quite a stir in Quebec. Russell was greatly insulted by Brant's allegations. Furthermore, the possibility of the Iroquois allying themselves with France alarmed everyone Liston wrote. Spain had just sided with France in its war with England, so it seemed to them as though the entire world were turning on the British. The Quebec officials all realized that the Iroquois were one ally the British could not afford to lose.

Russell invited Brant to meet with his executive council at York, the new capital of Lower Canada (today the province of Quebec), in June 1797. Russell was still waiting to hear from England about the deeds but hoped that the invitation would be enough of a show of good faith to avert any rash actions by Brant. Brant came away from this meeting with many assurances from Russell but remained worried that the Indians were still not being treated as independent peoples.

At a second meeting at York that same summer, Russell asked Brant for a written list of the lands to be sold and their purchasers. Once he received this, Russell said he could prepare the deeds. Brant wasted no time. He prepared the list according to Russell's instructions and then called a general council of Iroquois chiefs to sign the document. Three days later, Russell received the list and presented it to the council at York, which would decide whether to go ahead and okay the deeds or wait for official approval from England. Considering the urgent need to maintain a friendly alliance with the Indians, the council voted unanimously to approve the land sales and supply the deeds.

This vote was an important symbolic victory for Brant. The council's decision secured the Indians' right to negotiate their own land sales, thereby providing them with an independent source of income and making them less dependent on British presents and, consequently, less bound to obey British dictates. Russell recognized this as well as Brant and immediately attempted to curtail the Indians' newfound power by demanding that the Iroquois pay a fee to Canada each time they sold a tract of land.

Soon after the York council's vote, Russell at last received an answer from England about the deed question. In complete opposition to the council's decision, the Duke of Portland stated that the Iroquois had no power to sell land without the assent of the king. Portland instructed Russell to refund the money to the buyers of the Grand River land that Brant had sold and offer the Indians an annuity to match whatever they were paid for the land. The councilmen advised Russell to disregard Portland's order. Knowing of the possibility of the Indians allying themselves with France—of which Portland was ignorant—they thought it better to continue to appease the Indians.

Against the council's wishes, Russell broke the news to Brant as soon and as delicately as possible. Nevertheless, the Mohawk leader grew furious. He refused to accept the decision, refused the offered money, refused the annuity—he refused anything short of the confirming deeds. Russell himself described the scene in a letter to the Duke of Portland:

> I felt very unpleasantly at this moment. I was well aware that [Brant] was deeply committed; that he had great influence not only with his own tribe, but with the rest of the five nations . . . and that he was very capable of doing mischief.

Just as Brant was about to storm out of the room, Russell gave in. When Brant finally did leave Russell's office, he had in hand the documents confirming the past sales of the Grand River land and a title to the remaining land that enabled the Indians to use it as they wished. In addition, the Indians were no longer required to pay transfer fees to the British government.

The British would attempt to wrestle away the Mohawks' power to sell their land still one more time. Liston warned Brant that ministers in England were claiming that Haldimand's grant did not give the Indians the right to make land sales. Brant told Liston that all he ever wanted was for his people to hold land as they had before the American Revolution—land enough for all Iroquois Indians, land to use and land to sell, land to call their own.

Brant's old nemesis, John Simcoe, was largely responsible for convincing the British officials that it would be dangerous to allow the Indians to sell land to whomever they pleased. But Simcoe's efforts paled in comparison to Brant's perseverance. While Simcoe was making his case in England, Brant was rounding up surveyors, mapmakers, and land agents and putting them to work at Grand River. On February 5, 1798, armed with maps, deeds, Haldimand's grant, and his power of attorney, Brant met with Russell and the council at York. Before the day was out, Brant finalized the sales he had made nearly two years earlier and obtained five deeds for the Grand River settlement. All of Brant's buyers, as British subjects, were approved. One sale, to a John Docksteder, brought the Iroquois £39,867, the largest amount ever paid to Indians for land up to that time. Clearly, Brant knew the value of the land and had shrewdly negotiated the sales. At last, the Iroquois had a means to become self-sufficient once again.

Now that Brant had won possession of the Grand River land for his people, he returned to his home and went to work there with great energy. He began to build his own house along Burlington Bay (at present-day Burlington, Ontario), had a mill built on Grand River, and eventually obtained a bateau (a flat-bottomed boat), giving the community a way of traveling on Lake Ontario.

From time to time Brant was asked by other Indian leaders to advise them on their own land dealings. In one instance, Brant renegotiated the sale of the Missisaugas' land to the United States—land originally purchased at a criminally low price. Thereafter, the Missisaugas consulted Brant on nearly all their land deals.

Brant also gained a reputation as a friend to the poor. When some Indians at Grand River found themselves struggling to survive, Brant stepped in to help, providing flour, food, and other material goods. Brant was intent on proving that the Grand River settlement could survive and prosper without the aid of the British.

Unfortunately, he was perhaps a little bit too generous with the settlers at Grand River, especially those to whom he had sold tracts of land. By early 1798, all were in arrears on their land payments. The buyers were land speculators who had bought the land in hopes of a quick

An 1804 watercolor of the house Brant built on Burlington Bay. The structure was probably modeled after Johnson Hall, although it was far smaller and less grand. Nevertheless, the settlers in the area, most of whom lived in log cabins, took to calling the house "Brant's mansion" because it was so much more impressive than any other house they had seen.

resale and profit that never materialized. One of these buyers, Philip Stedman, was in debtor's prison in New York. With little or no money coming in from these sales, Brant was forced to sell still more land.

Angered by rumors that Brant was keeping the tenants' money for himself, some Grand River residents began to call for Brant's removal as the Mohawks' land agent. This group, consisting mostly of young warriors, complained to the Iroquois chiefs about Brant's management and succeeded in ousting him from his position. Although records show that Brant had not pocketed any of the money (he even lent money to the buyers to help them make their mortgage payments), he was never fully trusted again.

From this low point, things got even worse for Brant. Peter Hunter, a new lieutenant governor who had taken over in Quebec, forbade the Indians to sell their own land and refused to recognize the old sales. Brant went to see Hunter at once, but Hunter would not meet with him. Instead, Brant was told that Hunter was reviewing the land sales at Grand River and would settle the matter within two months. Of course, Hunter's inspectors found that all the buyers were in arrears and recommended that the Indians sue each of the tenants for the money owed. Brant came to the defense of one of his tenants, a man named Beasley, who had made every effort to keep up with his payments. Brant feared that Beasley would lose everything if he were sued.

In August 1803, a great council meeting was held at Niagara. Here, with the findings of Hunter's inspectors now known, the Iroquois chiefs who had accused Brant of stealing money had him reinstated as the Indians' land agent. But many still believed that Brant had become very rich by keeping profits from land sales for himself. These feelings were so widespread that the same chiefs once again deposed Brant a year later for alleged miscon-

This final portrait of Brant was made during his 1806 trip to Albany. The family with whom he was lodging suggested that he allow a local artist, Ezra Ames, to paint his likeness. Initially, Brant refused, maintaining that he should be shown wearing Indian regalia and that he had brought none with him. Only when his hosts provided him with an Indian-style calico shirt, necklace, and earring did he agree to sit for Ames.

duct. Brant fought this deposition and argued with Hunter that the Senecas and other Iroquois chiefs had no say in the land deals made at Grand River and no right to remove him as land agent.

Although he was unable to overturn this ruling, Brant continued to handle the land sales at Grand River. He did, however, sever all connections between the Grand River Mohawks and the other Iroquois. Brant's dream of a unified Indian confederacy had long since died, and he seems not to have regretted this final, permanent split with the Iroquois.

There was nothing for Brant to do now but wait for Hunter's decision and hope for the best. Surely, the situation looked grim. Despite Brant's earnestness, he had proved himself unfit to handle the buyers—none of the tenants had settled their accounts, and Brant was reluctant to remove them from the land.

For one last time, Brant decided to see what he could do. In early 1806, he sent a petition to the York assembly, asking for another review of the land-sales question. The petition was ignored until late that year, when the assembly voted to consider Brant's claims in its next session. Brant could wait no longer and vowed to go to England to speak with still more officials there. After collecting a number of debts, he raised enough money to begin his trip in August 1806. However, he got no farther than Albany, where he was unable to get the funds he needed to continue.

Back at Grand River, Hunter's inspectors finally came through with a settlement with the tenants. More than £9,000 had been collected and invested by the British government. From these investments, the Grand River Indians would receive a sizable sum of money annually. Hunter also had been in contact with a wealthy Scotsman named Lord Selkirk, who had agreed to purchase a large tract of land at Grand River. The profits from this sale would add substantially to the sum already obtained by the inspectors. Nearly 10 years after Brant began making land sales, the Mohawks were finally going to receive the fruit of his labor.

Late in 1807, while putting some finishing touches on the deed to Lord Selkirk, Brant became gravely ill. When the seriousness of Brant's condition became known, he had many visitors—Indian, American, and British. The last of these was John Norton, a former interpreter for the Mohawks and close friend of Brant's since 1793. To Norton, Brant spoke his final words before his death on November 24, 1807. He told Norton, "If you can get any influence with the great, endeavor to do [the Indians] all the good you can." No words could better express what Brant himself had strived to do throughout his life.

CHRONOLOGY

March 1743	Born somewhere in northeastern Ohio
1758	Fights for British in taking French-held Fort Ticonderoga
1759	Fights for British in siege at French-held Fort Niagara
1760	Serves as a member of Sir William Johnson's forces in attack on French fort at Montreal
1761	Begins lessons at Eleazar Wheelock's school for Indians in Lebanon, Connecticut
1763	Leaves school, plans to found mission at Oneida village of Oquaga
1765	Marries Peggie
1773	Marries Peggie's half sister Susanna three years after first wife's death
1775	Makes trip to England
1779	Marries Catharine Croghan, daughter of the head woman of the Mohawks, two years after death of Susanna
1783	Oversees establishment of Indian confederacy
1785	Makes second trip to England
1790	Brant and New York governor George Clinton reach agreement on Iroquois land sales
1792	Brant travels to Philadelphia to negotiate peace agreements with U.S. government
1793	Attends Maumee rapids conference and helps in negotiations for Indian land in the Ohio River country; succeeds in gaining a deed for Mohawk land at Grand River in Quebec
1795	Son Isaac dies from a head wound inflicted by Brant during an argument
1797	Brant travels to Philadelphia to meet with British ambassador to complain about restrictions on Indian land sales
1806	Tries to make a third trip to England but runs out of funds in Albany, New York
Nov. 24, 1807	Dies at his home in Brant's Town

FURTHER READING

Bonvillain, Nancy. *The Mohawk*. New York: Chelsea House, 1990.

Graymont, Barbara. *The Iroquois in the American Revolution*. Syracuse, NY: Syracuse University Press, 1972.

Jacobs, Wilbur R. *Dispossessing the American Indian: Indians and Whites on the Colonial Frontier*. Norman: University of Oklahoma Press, 1972.

Kelsay, Isabel Thompson. *Joseph Brant: Man of Two Worlds*. Syracuse, NY: Syracuse University Press, 1984.

O'Donnell, James. "Joseph Brant." In *American Indian Leaders: Studies in Diversity*, edited by R. David Edmunds. Lincoln: University of Nebraska Press, 1980.

Stone, W. L. *The Life of Joseph Brant-Thayendanegea*. 1838. Reprint. Saint Clair Shores, MI: Scholarly Press, 1970.

INDEX

PICTURE CREDITS

JONATHAN BOLTON holds a B.B.A. in marketing from the University of Miami, an M.A. in English from Brooklyn College, and is working towards a Ph.D. in English at the University of Maryland. He became interested in researching the life of Joseph Brant because he grew up in Mohawk country and spent part of his childhood in Brant Lake, New York, which was named for the Indian leader.

CLAIRE WILSON holds a B.A. in anthropology from Queens College and completed two years of graduate study, also in anthropology, at the State University of New York at Binghamton. She developed a deep interest in the life and history of the American Indian peoples during both her studies and her work on the INDIANS OF NORTH AMERICA series at Chelsea House Publishers. Wilson also wrote *Quanah Parker* in the NORTH AMERICAN INDIANS OF ACHIEVEMENT series.

W. DAVID BAIRD is the Howard A. White Professor of History at Pepperdine University in Malibu, California. He holds a Ph.D. from the University of Oklahoma and was formerly on the faculty of history at the University of Arkansas, Fayetteville, and Oklahoma State University. He has served as president of both the Western History Association, a professional organization, and Phi Alpha Theta, the international honor society for students of history. Dr. Baird is also the author of *The Quapaw Indians: A History of the Downstream People* and *Peter Pitchlynn: Chief of the Choctaws* and the editor of *A Creek Warrior of the Confederacy: The Autobiography of Chief G. W. Grayson.*